Toy Tips

A Parent's Essential Guide to Smart Toy Choices

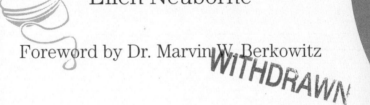

Marianne M. Szymanski
Ellen Neuborne

Foreword by Dr. Marvin W. Berkowitz

WITHDRAWN

JOSSEY-BASS
A Wiley Imprint
www.josseybass.com

Published by Jossey-Bass
A Wiley Imprint
989 Market Street, San Francisco, CA 94103-1741   www.josseybass.com

Jossey-Bass books and products are available through most bookstores. To contact Jossey-Bass directly call our Customer Care Department within the U.S. at 800-956-7739, outside the U.S. at 317-572-3986, or fax 317-572-4002.

Jossey-Bass also publishes its books in a variety of electronic formats. Some content that appears in print may not be available in electronic books.

Library of Congress Cataloging-in-Publication Data

Szymanski, Marianne M., date.
  Toy tips : a parent's essential guide to smart toy choices / Marianne M.
Szymanski, Ellen Neuborne ; foreword by Marvin W. Berkowitz.— 1st ed.
    p. cm.
  ISBN 0-7879-7436-6 (alk. paper)
  1. Toys. 2. Toys—Purchasing. 3. Child rearing. I. Neuborne, Ellen, date.
II. Title.
  GV1218.5.S99 2004
  649'.55—dc22

                                                        2004005547

Printed in the United States of America
FIRST EDITION
PB Printing   10 9 8 7 6 5 4 3 2 1

Contents

Disclaimer

Toy Tips® does not endorse or warrant any toy or product reviewed, nor is it responsible for any malfunction or injury associated with any toy mentioned. Options expressed and information provided serve solely to assist you in making informed purchasing decisions. When deciding on a toy or product for a child, be sure it is age appropriate for the child and used safely. Keep all toys with small parts away from young children. Toy Tips is completely independent and does not derive any income from manufacturers to review their products.

Foreword

What do we want for our children?

We want them to grow up happy. We want them to grow up healthy. And we want them to grow up to be people of good moral character.

More and more, as a society we are realizing the crucial necessity of character education. Although we have spent resources on improving the quality of academic education, the element of character education has often been overlooked. Too often, it is put aside as someone else's job. A school would consider it a parent's job. A parent might consider it the priority of a religious institution. And in the midst of this, children grow up, with the full force of our media culture around them, without society's many institutions contributing to the character of our children.

We must incorporate the building of moral competency into our child-raising priorities. A child's character education can be aided or hampered the day you buy his or her first toy. Learning is not just an activity of the classroom. In fact, some of the most important learning takes place far from the halls of traditional education. Learning begins at home and during play.

Play is a wonderful teacher. Through play, a child learns physical skills, language development, and social skills. Play shapes a child's personality and is part of the early material of moral character.

So it stands to reason that the type of play, and the toys involved, will matter a great deal. Research is clear on the impact of violent play. The physical skills it teaches are likely to be aggressive: how to hit and hurt others. The language acquired tends to be mean, hurtful, and crude. The social skills are often limited to resolving conflicts through fight or flight. The personality traits developed are antisocial, such as insensitivity to the pain of others and motivation to dominate. It's not a pretty picture.

Happily, the opposite is also true. When presented with prosocial toys and play, children are better able to emulate that behavior and follow a path to a more socially oriented personality. Toys that encourage sharing build generosity. Toys that allow for physical play without physical harm shape a character that is both strong and sensitive. Long before they enter a classroom, often before we realize it, children are playing and learning and developing the moral code that will guide them as adults.

What can we do to make early play a part of the development of strong moral character? We can take an active role in play and toy choices. We can encourage sports and rough-and-tumble play as outlets for high energy, but discourage pretend killing and hurting. We can buy our children toys that promote prosocial behaviors such as cooperation and healthy physical play. We can develop our own standards and values and apply them to play and toy choices. We can articulate those values to our children and to others around us.

Producing moral children of good character is not a quick process. Parents need to look at play and toys as parts of a child's moral development process. We need to come to our own judgments about what kinds of play and toys are appropriate and to act on those beliefs. It's more than just laying down rules. It is letting our children know what we stand for.

Marianne Szymanski, my former student, has had a passion for helping parents leverage the power of toys and play for the welfare of their children. She began this mission as a new college graduate over a decade ago and has only expanded it now that she is a mother herself. Her years of experience wedded with her passion for serving children and their parents make her a leading voice in the developmental benefits of toys and play. And she remains one of the few service-oriented, unbiased voices in this arena, something that is critically important to parents who are bombarded with sales messages, biased marketing pitches, and misinformation. This book is a great antidote to that cacophony.

Dr. Marvin W. Berkowitz
Sanford N. McDonnell
Professor of Character Education
University of Missouri-St. Louis

To our children:
Maximillian
Henry and Leslie

Preface
Why I Started Toy Tips

Thirteen years ago, Toy Tips was an idea in my head. I was working as a retail sales representative for a large international toy manufacturer, and my job was to sell and restock my company's products at mass-market toy stores. One day as I stood high on a ladder with a heavy box above my head, a grandmother asked me to help her choose some toys for her grandson's birthday.

At that point I realized that even though there were aisles and piles of toys everywhere, toy shoppers had little to guide them in making smart, fun choices for the children in their lives. That night, I went to the bookstore and purchased every magazine that offered any kind of advice about toys. I went to the library and checked out all the books I could find and started to read. Page after page, it all seemed the same: lots of information about toys, but no real advice on how, when, or why to buy them.

There was little statistical research. There were many "editor picks" and advice from "experts" who were paid by manufacturers to review and sometimes even promote selected toys. There were plenty of tests that relied on personal opinion, small groups of children, non-diverse demographics, interviews with nannies, and, in some cases, opinions from parents of no more than two families.

There were lists with promises but with no real information to back their claims. In some of the magazines, "Top Toys" lists were positioned near paid ads from the toy makers. What's a parent supposed to make of all this?

So I began my mission by developing my own research firm to test toys and uncover their value, without financial support or other input from the toy makers themselves. With the support of Dr. Marvin Berkowitz, Ph.D., a psychologist with a specialty in child development, and his colleagues, I created an academic, unbiased review process to learn the developmental benefits of toys and play. For thirteen years now, I have tested over thirty-four thousand toys with hundreds of thousands of children, using this unbiased research methodology to gain useful data.

This book furthers my mission by passing on the knowledge we have gained. My goal is to assist you in making informed purchasing decisions. You know your children best. You know what they are learning, what they are good at, and what skills they may need to work on. *Toy Tips* will turn you into your child's own personal toy expert. For relatives who may not see the children in their lives often and need help deciding what to buy, this book is for you too. And, parents-to-be, you will have a head start. Once you've learned the basics of smart toy choices, you can review the research results on hundreds of toys at www.toytips.com.

Remember, the toys you buy today will shape who your child will become tomorrow.

Acknowledgments

We would like to thank the thousands of children, teachers, parents, caregivers, and testing centers who have contributed to Toy Tips research studies over the years. Thank you to Dr. Marvin Berkowitz and Dr. James K. Giese for creating the testing methodology; to Dr. Scott Lange-necker and Cheri Riehle, OTR, for countless hours of true dedication; and to Marquette University and the University of Missouri-St. Louis, for their support. Thank you to our husbands, Garo and David, for their patience and support, and to our children, who give us ongoing insight. Thank you to our agent, Rick Broadhead, to Alan Rinzler and his team at Jossey-Bass, and to Marty Stein for his advice and encouragement. And finally, a special thank you to our parents, Jim and Marianne Szymanski and Burt and Helen Neuborne, for selecting our own special playthings, which entertained us, taught us, and helped us grow into the individuals we are today. Without you, this book would not be possible.

Marianne M. Szymanski
Founder, Toy Tips, Inc.
Milwaukee, Wisconsin

Ellen Neuborne
New York, New York

Toy Tips

Introduction

Why You Need a Toy Guide

Fretting is the national pastime of parenthood. We worry over everything, from schools and television to health and safety. Confronting our anxieties, we gobble up every bit of information and expert advice in hopes of making the best possible decisions for our children.

But in one crucial area, we parents remain surprisingly clueless: toys. Sure, we know the basics. Or we think we do. The truth is, the toy industry is one driven by hype and marketing savvy, and the average parent is at a distinct disadvantage. Toy buying seems like it ought to be child's play. But every grown-up who has stood dazed and confused in the aisle of a toy store or looked with despair at the overstuffed, overlooked toy box in the playroom knows better.

Often, toys are a mystery. How do you solve it? Knowledge is power, even in the playroom. Here's why you need a toy guide:

- **Because toys matter.** To you, they are little plastic or wooden playthings, diversions, gadgets, or trinkets. To a child, they are companions, prized possessions, even teachers and objects of inspiration. Toys play a central role in the life of a child, starting in infancy. They are a constant part of a child's experience. Think of all the time you spend considering the kind of education your child will need. That's important because education helps shape who a child will become. Toys play that role as well. They are part of the everyday environment that will sculpt your child's imagination, character, and outlook on life.

- ***Because the choices are overwhelming.*** Your average oversized toy retailer stocks hundreds of thousands of different items for sale. Then there are the discount stores, the specialty stores, the bookstores, and the video stores. To call the state of toy selection vast is an understatement. With so many choices, it's no wonder parents are confused. The sheer volume of selection is unnerving. Without guidance, you're lost in a sea of playthings.

- ***Because the advice out there is misleading.*** There are plenty of outfits out there ready to offer you a shortcut. There are many "Best Toys," "Top Toys," and "Favorite Toys" lists around. These and other experts say they'll take you past all the losers and straight to the best of the best toys. Problem is, many of those so-called experts have failed to disclose their biases. Look behind the curtain and you'll find that many an expert is actually on the payroll of a toy manufacturer. The only way to combat biased advice is with your own vault of knowledge.

- ***Because it's costing you money.*** The average parent shells out $300 a year on toys. What's that money getting you? Far too many savvy consumers seem to leave their wits at the door when they enter a toy store. A thinking adult who would never make an electronics purchase without carefully researching the options will drop down a credit card at a toy store solely on the strength of the marketing blurb on the box. That's your cash going out the door. How smart is that?

So take your first step toward confident toy purchasing. Educate yourself. Learn what the toy industry has to offer your child and how you can leverage those offerings to help create lasting positive play memories. Don't leave the task to your child. Kids are not the ones best equipped to choose the best toys. And certainly don't leave the choosing to the toy industry. They're in it to make money. The future of your child is *your* job. Yes, the task is daunting, but the cause is worthy, and you're the best one for the role. The toys you buy today will be part of your team. They will join you in the awesome task of raising a human being. Given the starring role toys play in a child's life, certainly it makes sense to choose those toys wisely. Your child is counting on you.

Chapter 1

Becoming Your Own Expert

So, you want to be a toy expert?

That's good. Every child needs a toy expert in his or her life. What's better, as a parent you are best suited to be your child's top toy expert. There's no one more qualified for the role.

Of course, that won't stop many others from trying to edge into your spotlight. One of the first lessons you'll learn on your road to personal toy expertise is how many would-be experts out there would love to sell you a short-cut. Perhaps the biggest growth area of the toy business in the last decade has been that of toy advice. From top ten lists to sticker awards on boxes to experts and gurus, the toy expert field is growing larger every year. And to a busy parent, it looks so inviting: a quick, simply packaged shortcut to great toy choices. It's an appealing sight.

Sadly, it's largely a mirage. You are the one suited to be the toy expert for your child. The advice market may offer nuggets and tidbits along the way, but it's up to the parent to make sense of it all. As you begin your quest for toy expertise, you can start by understanding what's wrong with most of the advice already out there and what little gems you might harvest from their offerings to make your own best choices.

The Trouble with Experts

Most of what passes for advice, especially during the holiday season, is mostly marketing, all wrapped up and nicely packaged for parents. Much of it is hopelessly biased. Some of it is just plain wrong. None of it substitutes for your own judgment of what makes a good toy for your child. The biggest mistake a parent can make during the holidays or any other toy shopping time is to rely on a list or award sticker to make a toy choice for a child. In many cases, these are nothing more than thinly disguised public relations campaigns designed to herd parents toward particular products. They are commercials dressed up in holiday finery.

Why Lists May Be Misleading

Every year, magazines, newspapers, and other media outlets put out stories that claim to have found the hot toys or, even worse, the best toys for the holiday season. These lists set out to highlight certain toys as better than the rest. Very few of them attain that goal.

The problems:

- *Journalists know journalism.* Many of the editors and reporters involved are not experts in psychology or education or child development. The opinion of the average journalist—even if that individual is a parent or grandparent—is no better or worse than the opinion of your neighbor.
- *Magazines want to sell magazines.* So their "Hot Toys" or "Best Toys" lists are going to reflect that goal. The toys will be chosen for the story with an eye toward what the readership wants to see—and that's not necessarily the full universe of available toys. Any publication's toy story will be shaped by the demographics of its readership. They may or may not dovetail with the demographics of your own family.

TOY TIP

What are these magazine and newspaper lists good for? News. If you want to know what is new this year, you want to peruse these lists. They don't have the expertise to tell you whether the toys are good or bad, but they can reliably tell you about new products the major toy makers have to offer.

- *Publications have advertisers.* And the advertisers are often toy companies. Some publications will handle their toy stories separately from their advertisers. Others, particularly trade or other industry publications, may be directly influenced to feature toys from their best advertising customers. Many publications offer their own awards based on their own criteria. Take a closer look and you'll see it is most likely an opinion poll from a nondiverse sample of parents or staffers.

What the Kids Don't Know

Contrary to popular belief, children are not toy experts. They are toy consumers. But that doesn't prevent everyone from TV stations to parenting magazines setting up child-centered "toy tests" during the holiday season. They are billed as the best way to find the best toys. Not so.

The problems:

- *Expertise is by its nature an adult attribute.* Knowledge of educational value, developmental appro-

TOY TIP

Although lots of toy tests are problematic, every once in a while you can come across a good one that really cuts through the marketing mayhem and analyzes toys. Check the methodology of these child-centered tests. If they are run by qualified educators and the testing population is diverse— that is, not limited geographically, economically, or culturally—you may glean some good information.

priateness, and hidden flaws are complicated concepts best understood by adults. Who would trust a child to look at a toy and determine its safety or educational value? Qualified adults are the best judges of toys, just as they are the best judges of automobiles or consumer products. Just because a child may ultimately be the end user does not mean a child is the best judge of the product.

- **Where's the science?** In many cases, child-centered testing is done in a way that is at best unscientific and at worst completely random. Some tests are set up in day care centers. That already limits the results to children of a certain socioeconomic status—those whose parents can afford day care. Other tests are arranged in an "open play" setting with little in the way of parameters. That may make for good television, but it doesn't get you any closer to knowing which are the best toys.
- **Who's running the test?** A true test—one designed to produce accurate and substantive data—should be

administered by an experienced researcher. In the case of toys, you'd want to see someone with a background in education or child psychology to ensure that the adult in the room is not influencing the results. With many child-centered toy tests, that's hardly the case. Tests are run by everyone from day-care teachers to individual families to publicists for toy manufacturers.

Who's Paying Your Expert?

These days, everybody's an expert. We live in a society where expertise is prized. And in every industry, individuals are encouraged to flaunt their expertise and hang out a shingle declaring their willingness to share this inside knowledge with others. For a price. Expertise is a booming industry, and the toy industry is not an exception. The marketplace is full of people with toy knowledge for sale. But the buyer should beware.

The problems:

- *It's a business.* It's not uncommon for people interviewed on TV or by the print media to be positioned as "experts" but actually be paid spokespeople. Toy companies make financial arrangements with toy "experts" all the time so that their wares will be mentioned in interviews. Your "expert" may have a conflict of interest in the form of his or her paycheck.
- *It's show business.* When was the last time you saw a dull guru on TV? Often, an expert gets airtime based on his or her ability to perform on TV. It's a fact of the business. So the advice you're getting may not necessarily be from the most intelligent or well-informed guru. Instead, you need to understand that what you're

TOY TIP

True toy experts are not necessarily limited to talking about the newest toys on the market. Many will discuss toy choices that include classics as well as newcomers. So by listening to an expert talk about toy choices, you may actually get a broader perspective than you might from other sources.

getting is the most telegenic toy guru. That's the impact television has had on the advice business.

The Reality of Retailing

Toy stores often put out their own lists of top toys. These are generally designed to boost traffic into the retail store. Toy stores may set up their own in-house tests or simply issue press releases with their top picks.

The problems:

- ***Depending on when the toy store list emerges, there may or may not be any real sales data behind it.*** A list that appears early in the season—say, September or October—is probably based on the retail buyer's best guess. Consumers may take a different path.
- ***Toy stores must move inventory.*** Their lists are naturally going to promote the items they hope to sell. When they say "best toy" they really mean "toy we'd most like to see move off our shelves."

TOY TIP

Stores are the best gauges of actual popularity. Toy experts may say a particular plaything is hot, but the proof comes when the cash register rings. Toy retailer data, especially data based on real retail sales and that appear in the heart of the shopping season—say, November or December—are going to offer you actual insight into what is most popular this year.

- ***Retailers have specific demographics.*** A specialty toy store may issue a list that encompasses the high-end toys that it stocks. A discount chain will feature a completely different set of mass-market toys. Neither embraces the full universe from which a shopper can choose.

Stop the Stickers!

See those award stickers plastered all over the toys in your local store? Ignore them. One of the biggest growth segments of the toy industry in recent years has been toy awards. Although a few toy awards seem prestigious and worthwhile, most are simply another attempt at marketing, and there's little but business interest behind them.

The problems:

- ***What does the sticker really tell you?*** Not much. No entry rules. No judging criteria. No information on whether or not the manufacturer has paid to receive

TOY TIP

Some awards have enough history (over ten years) to be legitimate helpmates in the search for great playthings. If you are able to easily uncover the award criteria and the award isn't paid for or biased, you have a nugget of value.

consideration or placement by the sticker giver. The toy award business is unregulated, so toy award givers can devise any system they like. As a consumer, you have little idea what's behind that sticker. And if you did know, you'd be shocked. Plenty of award programs are cash deals. Many require "submission fees," which biases the results right then and there. Toy makers pay for consideration. What you envision as a detailed judging process may actually be little more than a business transaction.

- *Just because someone else judged it a great toy doesn't mean you'll agree.* Don't assume that a toy judge—even a qualified one—knows best. You're the best judge for your child.
- *Toy makers leverage these award stickers for good shelf placement.* It's all part of the retail process. You see the stickers because they are part of the marketing program. Consider them tiny sticky commercials.

When the News Isn't News

Every year, the media manage to come up with stories about holiday toys. Often, the story centers around a hot or "must-have" toy. Kids are interviewed asking for the toy.

TOY TIP

When watching the news, pay more attention to stories with statistics or credentials to back up assertions. These will give you a good idea of what's really going on with their reviews and toy tests.

Parents are interviewed in their harried search for the toy. Retailers give quotes about how this toy is hot, hot, hot. Annual coincidence? Nah. These stories are perennials.

The problems:

- **Is it really news?** No. It's just the tyranny of the calendar. The holiday season goes into full swing, and media outlets, from national television to local newspapers, dig around for a good holiday toy story.
- **Does it love the camera?** A reality of the news business is that it often revolves around what looks good on the page or screen. Toys that photograph well are likely to turn up in these stories.
- **Is it dramatic?** News outlets like drama. And if there isn't much, they'll add some. A toy may not really be in short supply nationwide, but that won't stop a local news crew from interviewing a frantic mother unable to find the toy.

Industry Gossip

Unwilling to sit on the sidelines during the crucial toy-selling season, toy industry associations have jumped into the media mix, setting up their own press confer-

TOY TIP

Industry association events are essentially trade shows. As such, they are good for a broad look at the newest wares of the industry.

ences, awards systems, and lists to generate sales for their membership.

The problems:

- ***Often, industry association events are billed as an "inside scoop."*** In fact they are simply the consolidated message of its members. Look at them as commercials from toy companies.
- ***Associations work for their members, not for consumers.*** You're unlikely to get any negative spin from an industry event.
- ***Associations are for members only.*** Don't bother trying to find information about a toy made by a small company that's not a member of the large association.

Conclusion

It's hard to say no to so many offers of advice. But keep in mind that lists and awards and experts can offer only guides and suggestions. Ultimately, you'll need to be the one educated and savvy enough to make toy choices for your child. Resist the urge to follow shortcuts when it comes to finding the best toys. Your best route to toy happiness is not via a guru or top ten list. It's through your own knowledge of your child and of what the toy industry has to offer.

WORKSHEET

Toy Test Red Flags

Trying to determine if the test or list you're perusing is valid? Ask these key questions:

- Do companies pay an entrance fee to have their toys considered? That's already a conflict. The test is relying on its participants for funds.
- How many toys were tested? Of those, how many were recommended? If everyone in the test gets recommended, that's a red flag.
- If there's an expert panel of judges, what are their credentials? Look for people whose expertise you would trust. Individual opinions from parents and teachers aren't research.
- Are the judges paid for their participation? That's not necessarily a bad thing, but you should know who is writing the check.
- Was the test conducted by an education or research professional? Tests run by journalists and publicity coordinators may be inaccurate.
- How large was the sample of children in the test? A small group will yield less reliable results.
- Was the sample of children demographically diverse? Race and gender are not the only factors. Look also for economic and geographic diversity in a testing sample.

Tales from the Toy Tips Lab

"Do you like this toy?" Ask a small child with a toy in his hand, and chances are excellent that he will say yes. Why? Because he wants to keep playing. That's the natural reaction of a child and a very good example of why child-centered toy tests are often far off base. Every year I watch with dismay as television stations and magazines set up toy tests. They round up a bunch of children, hand out the toys, and ask them "Do you like these toys?" Sure they do! They all say yes. But the test is meaningless. The TV stations have done nothing more than prove that kids at play want to keep playing and not give the toys back. Over the years, I've worked to develop research methods that uncover the value of toys and the reactions children have to specific toys. But I've learned that asking a child to express like or dislike for a toy isn't a useful research methodology. A toy in the hand is a good thing. Kids will nod politely at the questioning adult and then go right back to playing.

Chapter 2

Toy Types

According to the Toy Industry Association, there are 104 kinds of toys on the market today. That's 104 different product categories, ranging from blocks and puzzles to dolls and board games. Each category has within it hundreds, even thousands of different items—a dizzying array for anyone entering a toy store. As you walk through the door and stand at the front, even trying to decide which aisle you want is a big choice.

So it helps to know your toy types. Although the toy industry may look to the casual observer like a haphazard collection of playthings, it is organized by category, and a little knowledge of the industry sorting system can help guide you in your buying and ultimately your playtime. By understanding how the industry arranges its categories, you'll be better able to make your own call.

Are any categories strictly off-limits? Not at all. Don't believe everything you read in the media—no category of toy is all bad. At any given time, it may be popular to criticize traditional dolls or action figures or video games. But in fact, every toy category has its pros and cons and ultimate play value. The key is to make an informed choice and follow through by encouraging, modeling, and even getting down on the playroom floor and participating in appropriate play.

Start by knowing your categories.

Indoor Toys

Too often, indoor time for a child means time in front of the television set. One way to avoid this bad habit is to be sure you have on hand a good selection of indoor toys. These are toys whose materials and play patterns are best suited to a playroom or family room. They may vary greatly with the age of the child, but their overall purpose is the same: to foster creative and entertaining playtime. Your smart choices in this category can lead to great indoor play habits throughout childhood.

Stuffed Toys

You can always spot the nonparents at a baby shower. They're the ones who bought teddy bears for the newborn. One of the first rules of the stuffed toys category is that plush is not a good buy for very tiny babies. Some background is necessary for navigating this popular if somewhat misunderstood aisle of the toy store.

Benefits   When properly chosen, these soft and cuddly toys do much more than dress up a nursery. They take on important developmental roles in a child's life. They are vehicles to teach imaginative play and role playing. They are objects on which to lavish affection and loving care. They take on status as companions and comfort objects. They are often the first toys on which a child bestows the ultimate compliment of "favorite," and more than a few adults have secreted away in the back of their closets the stuffed animal from childhood that is lovingly remembered as the first best friend. Stuffed toys are objects of true emotional connection.

Timing   So when should teddy make his appearance? When baby sits up. Before a child has reached that physical milestone, stuffed toys can actually be hazardous and shouldn't be put in a young infant's crib. Once baby is more mobile, some of the safety issues are overcome, although you must still carefully inspect any stuffed toy for loose or glued-on elements. Get rid of them before giving the stuffed toy to a small child.

At this age, often in the second half of the first year, a baby will start to show interest in a stuffed toy. You may use it to engage baby in peekaboo or other interactive games. Keep in mind that your little one is most interested in your participation in this game, and any stuffed toy makes a lovely prop, not a substitute for you.

When a child reaches the toddler stage, stuffed toys take on a far more significant role. The toddler years are the golden age of stuffed toys. This is the age of make-believe, the time when stuffed toys come alive. A toddler may have a favorite among a collection of stuffed toys, or will lavish attention on a single one. Look for a stuffed toy that a small child can easily handle. An oversized gorilla may get a great initial reaction when you walk through the door with it, but if the child can't control it, carry it around, position it, and in general have mastery over it, its play value is diminished. Besides, where are you going to store these stuffed monstrosities? The best stuffed toys fit under the average toddler's arm.

What about older kids? That's very much a personality call. As kids reach school age, stuffed toys are not as easy a pick. Some kids will still be happy to play with them, others will write them off as baby toys. You need to think through the play patterns of the child in question to make a good choice. Is this a child who is excited by fantasy play? Does the child like to act out scenes and corral any available participants into the production? A quality stuffed toy may still be welcome. Also, some kids enjoy

TOY TIP

Stuffed toys are great for the imagination. Encourage your child to pretend and to act out a variety of stories. You can let the child lead the way on some and suggest others of your own. If your child has a favorite stuffed toy, get out another from the toy box and engage in some pretend play—make up funny voices for your own toy and model the role-play behavior. Don't let any preordained story lines or character traits restrict your play. In the land of make-believe, dinosaurs can teach school, turtles can be ballerinas, and teddy bears can live in the sea. Also, listen to your child's pretend play scenarios. Often they give clues as to what is going on in your little one's mind. Is she afraid of the dark? Worried about an upcoming trip? Unhappy with the latest snack selections? You may hear these opinions come out as the child interacts with a favorite stuffed toy.

collecting various lines of stuffed toys, so that's an obvious use for plush as well.

Warning   Safety is a key concern for babies and small children. Never keep stuffed toys in a crib with a newborn. They should stay on the shelf as nursery decor until baby can sit up and roll over with ease. Also, for any child under three, beware of anything that can come off the toy—such as glued-on eyes—because they may be a choking hazard.

In addition to the safety hazards, stuffed toys present some unique health issues. Be sure you wash and dry your stuffed toys regularly—once every three months is a good rule of thumb. If your toy is not machine washable, at least send it through a spin in the dryer. That will help reduce its dust quotient. Keep in mind that stuffed toys are quite good at collecting allergens, such as pet dander, dust, and germs from eager toddler hands and mouths. If your child is sneezing a lot, consider sending teddy and his friends through a wash and dry cycle. That may go a long way toward reducing any allergens.

Construction Toys

From blocks to bricks to model cities, construction toys offer a wide variety of play options. The littlest ones will enjoy the build-up, knock-down play pattern, and an older child may work for hours to create a masterpiece.

Benefits It's hard to beat the construction toy for play value. The list of benefits is long. Good construction toys help build fine motor skills. They encourage concentration and creativity. The same toy can foster both independent play and educational teamwork. They open possibilities for pretend play and, perhaps best of all from an adult perspective, they can be good for hours, months, even years of fun. It's not unusual for a favorite construction toy to be in use for several years over a childhood and passed down to younger siblings. Talk about getting your money's worth.

That said, there are plenty of ways to make mistaken choices when it comes to construction toys. And nothing is more frustrating than seeing a potentially fun, educational, and enduring toy sit ignored on the shelf. It happens

TOY TIP

Once anything is built—whether it's a farm made up of blocks or an elaborate plastic brick landscape—make a big deal out of the finished project. Admire it, put it on display in the family room for others to enjoy, take a picture of your child with it. Resist the urge to ask, "What is it?" Some of the little ones will immediately read that you can't tell by looking. Instead go for the more neutral "Tell me all about this!" You'll get all the information you need. Part of what makes a construction toy a great buy is the continued skill development it can enhance. By showing approval and enthusiasm, you encourage your child to tackle additional, even more complicated construction projects and build on his or her skills.

a lot with construction toys. Despite their many benefits, there are plenty of pitfalls.

Timing   Often the earliest age for a construction toy is about eighteen months. Even when babies are just pushing the items around, they are moving toward their early construction skills. For little ones, you're looking for big chunky items that stack or fit together easily. Very easily. Preschoolers can handle plastic blocks that click together or other, more complicated items. Remember that very small pieces are a choking hazard for children under three. You should be willing to demonstrate and coach these early construction efforts, but don't get pressed into putting the whole thing together yourself. A team effort is a great play idea, but you want your little one to have as much of the hands-on as possible. If he or she can't handle the motor work required, you may want to put the toy away for a few months and try later.

Once a child reaches school age, you can look into the more elaborate sets that may depict castles or monuments or space stations. Depending on your child's personality, these sets can lead to hours of independent play or enjoyable rainy-day family projects. Try both scenarios with your child and see which one seems to bring out the best in your child's play. Invest in resealable bags to hold all the pieces—few toy manufacturers design their packaging with long-term storage in mind, and pieces often get lost.

Warning   One of the most common errors of a parent in the construction toy aisle is to muse, "Oh, my child is so smart. I'll get the BIG set." This is often a BIG mistake. The size of the construction toy you purchase is not a referendum on whether or not your child is destined for Harvard. In fact, a poor choice in this category can set your child back some. If you bring home a complicated or hard-to-finger construction set and present it with glee and anticipation, your four year-old will likely dive right in. And if he or she can't manage it because it's not developmentally appropriate, the child may think, "What's wrong with me?" The advice for most parents is, think about what kind of construction toy your child can handle and then take one step down on that developmental ladder. You will do far better picking a toy that is slightly easy rather than a toy that is too hard.

Dolls

There's so much variety within the doll category that it hardly makes sense to try to collect them all into one section of the toy store. Dolls are a multifaceted group. There are baby dolls; character dolls; big dolls; small dolls; dolls that do things; dolls with hair; dolls that sit on shelves and look pretty; dolls that never leave their boxes, collecting value; dolls of plastic, wood, stuffing, and china. The choices go on.

Dolls are also a category with a bit of controversy. Although few suggest that dolls are to blame for gender inequality among adults, some experts do say that gender roles—such as those that cast girls as nurturers and boys as actors—are perpetuated by doll play. What do you do? As with any toy category, the key is not to avoid or blot out but to make smart choices and model the kind of behavior you want to see develop in your child. Dolls have many pluses going for them, and there's no reason politics should get in the way for either girls or boys.

Benefits   What can dolls teach? They are marvelous for fostering nurturing, pretending, and role playing. Many dolls that come with hair or clothing can help build fine motor skills. Dolls are also a great way to gain insight into the inner world of the preschooler or young child. How a child plays with a doll, talks to a doll, and has the doll act can be a true window into the issues a child is experiencing. A child with a brand-new younger sibling may act out baby-care scenarios. One who just went on a trip may recreate the experience with dolls as actors. Children may gather in a pair or in groups and use dolls as their proxies to act out their own social issues. It makes sense to pay attention to doll play, as it is often a child's way of expressing hopes, fears, and desires.

Timing   Dolls will become most attractive in the preschool years, as children begin to act out stories from both their fantasies and real life and look to dolls to act as their proxies. This is an age when it is perfectly appropriate for both girls and boys to play with dolls. More than a few dads and grandpas will blanche at the sight of a little boy playing with a doll. But honestly, it's merely a reflection of the times. Today, a little boy might well see his father as a full partner in child care. He may have many times seen and experienced his father in a nurturing role, so it is perfectly normal and appropriate for him to act out that very accurate scenario with a doll. Dads today are very involved in nurturing, perhaps more so than they were in previous generations. Although adults today may not have seen their own fathers change diapers, push a stroller, or feed the baby, today these sights are quite common. The little boy who plays with a doll is appropriately modeling the behavior he sees in men today. Don't worry, and tell any worried relatives to relax.

Warning   Dolls that do a trick—cry, sing, even go potty—are often heavily promoted on television and can be seen as highly desirable by young children. You can't blame the kids—these are sophisticated marketing campaigns and are designed to spark intense lobbying. What should you do? First off, this is a good time to explain to a child—even a preschooler—that we don't buy everything we see on TV and that sometimes, toys on TV commercials aren't really all that much fun in real life. Your children may not always believe you, but it's important that you say this to them

TOY TIP

As a parent or caretaker, you can use a doll to model behavior you'd like to see. You may use the doll to demonstrate empathy or concern or appropriate social greetings. Dolls make terrific teaching tools.

early and often. The marketers are making a very strong pitch to your kids, and it's crucial that you get in equal time with your view on a doll that turns a cartwheel or sucks her thumb. What's more, these dolls can have very limited play spans. The novelty element is entertaining, but once that wears off, the doll is shelved. So be judicious in your choice of novelty dolls. Once in a while you may see it as an appropriate choice. But beware the urge to take on a new doll each time manufacturers are able to come up with a new trick. That's an endless cycle, and what it really teaches kids is the enormous power of marketing.

Cartoon Toys

If you can hardly remember having a TV-themed toy as a child, it's no wonder. They were just a small slice of the toy industry in previous generations. Today they are a driving force, and your children are well aware of the size and scope of television's influence. Toys based on television or other entertainment characters fall into the industry category called licensed merchandise, and it's a multibillion-dollar business worldwide.

Benefits   No, licensed toys are not all bad. Just because a character appears on TV doesn't mean it can't dole out positive influence as a toy. One obvious pro to a licensed toy: chances are good your child will recognize the character. If you've purchased an educational game or toy that you hope will teach a skill, pairing it with a character the child already likes is a wise move. No need to sell the child on the benefits of playing with a toy that teaches early reading skills or helps build fine motor coordination if that lovable TV character is doing all the work for you. An educational toy is not diminished because it has a recognizable character on it. If it's a good toy and really does teach a skill, and if it's developmentally appropriate, the licensed character packaging does not undermine the benefit.

Also, some licenses simply expand the reach of truly beloved and wonderful children's characters. Characters from classic fairy tales and traditional children's literature can come to life for a new generation through a carefully constructed licensing program. If your child has learned to recognize a character because it is now in a licensed stuffed animal or video or other toy, take the opportunity to bring in the character's roots by reading to your child the original story or poems.

Timing   Any time is fine to introduce an entertainment-themed toy, but make sure the toy you choose has an age-appropriate story line. Don't assume that because the toy is based on a cartoon character it is an appropriate choice for kids. In fact, many cartoons today are designed for older kids or even teens, and their themes are far too mature for a preschooler or toddler, so a stuffed icon from one of those shows is probably not a great choice. For

TOY TIP

One other note on licensed toys: your child may ask for them often, and that's because the marketing and advertising of these toys is quite prevalent. But kids don't always know exactly what they want. When your child asks for a particular character doll or book or board game, listen carefully and consider agreeing to the category request. Your child may simply want to play with that type of toy, and happens to know the licensed character's name from television or other ad messages. Don't stop listening the minute you hear the character's name—there may be a broader request on the table. And it may be a choice you're both happy with.

small children, stick to the characters based on the entertainment made for them. That's a good match.

Warning   If there's one corporate player trying its best to undermine your careful choice of licensed toys, it's the fast food industry. Burger chains have become particularly adept at latching on to the latest Hollywood offering and shooting out plastic doodads in kids' meals. And these toys come complete with a large side of television advertising. This minefield requires some careful parental navigation. Again, although your children may not completely understand you, it pays to explain the fact that the burger chains are using these toss-away toys to get you into their restaurants. Certainly school-age or older kids can be expected to begin understanding the concept of a promotional come-on. Although you may occasionally feel it's fine to eat fast food and pick up a cheap plastic toy in the process, you may not want to make this a habit. It's neither nutritionally nor educationally sound.

Puzzles

Puzzles are sort of like new foods: you can't really tell if the child is going to like them until he or she tries them. It's very hard to spot a "puzzle person" otherwise. The best advice on puzzles is to dive right in with one or two and see how it goes.

Benefits   Puzzles help build fine motor skills, they challenge a child to develop acuity in spatial relations, and they can be both independent and group activity toys. For some kids, puzzles become a true passion that can extend well into adulthood. What's more, puzzles offer a great opportunity for a family activity. A complicated puzzle can involve even young children when it's played as an intergenerational family game.

Timing   First puzzles for toddlers should be the sturdy peg-piece variety, in which each piece comes with a small handle for easy maneuvering. These first puzzles teach the basic spotting skills of puzzle play: How can I tell where this piece goes? At first, your child may not use his or her eyes to work the puzzle and will simply try each hole and each piece. But eventually the idea of looking first will catch on. That's an important developmental leap. Demonstrate the puzzle yourself, but then step back and let your little one handle the pieces and figure it out. That's when

TOY TIP

If your child doesn't seem to like puzzles, don't push it. Some personalities just aren't suited to the task. But don't give up entirely on the category. A child that rejects puzzles at age four may warm to them at age six or seven. If you get a "no" at first, fall back and make a note to try again at a later age. Because they are rarely advertised on television, puzzles are the kind of toy that often an adult must offer before a child makes the toy connection.

the learning is taking place, and it's a true moment of mastery when a little one can eyeball a puzzle.

From that first stage, you might want to move on to two-together puzzles—where pieces fit in pairs. That's often popular with the two- to four-year-old set. When your child is about age four, you can start to expect a broader understanding of the toy and move on to the early jigsaw puzzle types. Licensed characters or familiar objects like a fire truck or dog make good choices. If the child can have a mental image of the finished puzzle, that will help. And if the puzzle forms the face of a beloved character, that's a bonus for a preschooler.

Warning   Know your puzzle materials. Puzzles come in a wide variety, and your choice depends on the amount of use you expect the toy to take. For a household of school-age children, the average cardboard piece puzzle is safe, but one with preschoolers or toddlers may benefit from puzzles made of wood, plastic, even foam. They'll hold up better. For children under age three, beware small pieces or delicate pieces that can become small when ripped to shreds by tiny toddler hands.

Board Games

This classic category has something for almost every age and interest. You may find that some of your old favorites from childhood are still around, and there are also many new titles on store shelves.

Benefits   As soon as you've got "two or more players" you've got a teaching tool. The nature of board games makes them highly instructive. Sitting across from a friend or parent, a child learns to take turns, strategize, deal with winning and losing, and, perhaps most important, engage in the social interaction of playing with another person or even a group. Also, board games provide a setting useful for discussion and teaching. When you're out on the playground with other kids and other parents, it's hard to get your little one's ear to discuss the finer points of turn taking. But bring out a board game and sit just the two of you on the floor for some one-on-one playtime, and you'll be sure to get a greater share of your child's attention.

Timing   At what age should you introduce a board game? A two-year-old may be ready to tackle the concept of turn taking, and a board game designed for a toddler is a great way to teach this skill. Repetition is key. As you play, say over and over, "It's my turn," "It's your turn." This is an advanced concept, and your toddler may not get it right away. Use your hands, demonstrate, and say aloud what's going on. Remember, it's not in a toddler's nature to hand over a toy or step back and let another take a turn. You need to model this action—often—throughout the game. Don't worry that you're overdoing it. It may take a while for the "my turn, your turn" concept to take hold. But it's an important one, and board games can make this key teaching moment more fun.

There are two kinds of board games: those based on skill and those based on chance. Don't assume that skill games are only for older kids. There are skill games for preschoolers, just geared to preschool skills such as memory. Read the box carefully, and if you can, read the game directions. That will give you a good sense of how hard the game is and whether or not your child will be able to play along. Most major game makers list age ranges on their packaging—those are just guidelines. Every child is different. If the game involves reading or basic math skills, you'll want to have it for a school-age child. Games for younger kids should be heavily visual.

As children reach school age, board games take on important social roles with peers. A collection of fun, age-appropriate board games can help make for a great play date. Knowledge of classic board games, such as checkers, as well as those from major toy companies is useful social currency. Playing these games with your child and encouraging your child to play them with friends help facilitate this aspect of social growth.

Board games are a toy category that can comfortably extend well into later childhood and even the teen years. There are many board games that are quite complex, calling for skill, strategy, teamwork, and knowledge. Games that challenge players to answer questions, come up with strategies, or work as a team are often very popular even

TOY TIP

When it comes to skill games, should you let your child win? Sure, sometimes. Obviously most adults will be able to beat a child at a skill-based game, and losing all the time is no fun at all. But winning and losing are part of life. So letting your child win all the time doesn't do him or her any great favors. The best advice for parents is to let your child win some games and model the kind of language and behavior you'd like to see in your child. Use words and phrases a child can understand, and maintain your sense of humor. Your child will take cues from you. Do this often and in a variety of games so that your message can sink in.

with older kids. Choose the game carefully to be sure it won't be brushed off as a "baby toy." Packaging will be important here—older kids will take their cues from the box graphics. Does it look like complicated, sophisticated fun? That will help make the sale. And a challenging board game can be a great way to connect with your rapidly maturing offspring.

Warning   If the game is based on chance, not on skill, it may be important to explain this to your child, particularly if he or she is a natural perfectionist. Some children may become upset when they do everything "right" yet still lose. If it's a game of chance, say so. That will help your child process the outcome of the game.

Action Figures

When one particular action figure first came to fame one Christmas season, not all the reception was positive. While some parents hustled to snag the hard-to-find toys as holiday gifts, others complained that their kids were engaging in a lot more playground kicking—the signature move of the action heroes—and suggested that the toys were to blame. That's just one example of the controversy that has sprung up around action figures. For tiny plastic toys, action figures stir up adult-sized passions.

Benefits   Yes, there are good reasons to embrace action figures. The key is knowing what those reasons are and how to leverage them. The good news about action figures: they encourage pretend play, role playing, and social interaction. That's no small set of benefits, especially considering the market that most appreciates them—little boys. One of the great disservices done to boys growing up in our time is that early in their preschool and school-age years, we begin to tell them that pretend play is somehow better suited to girls, and we guide them toward sports, games, and other competitive activities. There's nothing wrong with a boy who likes games, but there's quite a bit of developmental benefit to young boys' playing out scenes and acting out stories with their own representatives. If dolls and stuffed animals don't appeal, you'll find that these boys pick up their action figures for the roles. In this vein, action figures are a great teaching tool. They offer an opportunity for social interaction with other kids and a platform for creative play. Also, many action figures come with detailed story lines, and play with

TOY TIP

If your child is interested in an action figure, your first job is to learn the story behind it. Watch the cartoon, read the comic book, rent the video. Whatever it is that tells the story of the figure, you need to check it out and understand what the action figure is all about. This is important because if you give your child an action figure, he or she is probably going to act out the story line. So you need to decide whether or not you will be comfortable with that. And don't assume that just because you don't watch the show at home, your child is oblivious to the action figure's history. Kids know all about this stuff—they hear it from each other, from older siblings, from kids on the playground. You need to know this story, and if you decide to buy the toy, discuss it with your child. Children need to understand how what they see their favorite action figures doing does or does not fit in with real life. Action figures provide an excellent foil for discussing your own family values. What do these characters do that we admire? What things do we not do in our family that are just fine in action figure land? What is fine for make-believe characters but not OK for real people?

a particular figure can lead the child to buy books or comic books with the same character, encouraging reading and other activities.

Timing   Toddlers may enjoy the occasional action figure, but passions really take off for preschool and school-age kids. They're at an age when action figures and their popularity spring out of the social fabric of school life. In many cases, a child will gravitate to a particular hero or story line rather than to the entire category of action figure toys.

Warning   Let's face it: action figures just aren't warm, fuzzy, let's-talk-about-this fellows. As their name implies, they are characters of action. In many cases, this action is violent. Depending on the character, it can be kicking and punching, organized fighting, or all-out warfare. These are characters that lash out rather than sit down for a group hug. As a parent, you need to make the call as to what level of this behavior you find acceptable. For some parents, it's none at all; for others, it's fine so long as it's confined to the world of make-believe and no real people get hurt.

Activity Toys

Activity toys are a complex category. They run a very broad gamut, from stacking toys for toddlers to craft toys for older children. Many parents pass them by because they seem to offer little in the way of ongoing use. Often they are toys that offer a craft or other activity, and once the supplies are used up that's the end. Sometimes it's even a one-shot toy: make the one item, and that's all.

But don't let the lack of longevity fool you. Activity toys have a lot to offer, and they're often a smart choice even if they can't hang around to be handed down through the generations.

Benefits   Depending on the toy, activity toys promote a variety of positive skills. They can build fine motor skills, inspire creativity, encourage independent play, and even introduce a child to new styles of artwork. A child may first discover something like needlepoint, knitting, or pottery through an activity toy. Never underestimate a toy's ability to open a new door.

Timing   Although many activity toys are designed with school-age kids in mind, there are plenty for younger children as well. The first thing to keep in mind is the skill level necessary to complete the task. Although it's fine and even good to participate with a child on an activity project, you should not be doing all the work. So look for activity toys with projects that look doable. There are many geared for small children, such as a plate or cup design project or handprint cast. You want the toy to be interesting without being frustrating, so read the packaging carefully and try to envision your child going through each of the steps. If more than two or three sound too hard, you may want to step down a bit in difficulty.

Warning   Beware the desire to overspend. A good activity toy can range from $10 to $20. If you want to spend more on a toy that you hope will produce something truly spectacular, that's fine. But it's not a requirement for this category.

TOY TIP

Be prepared to sit down with the child and fully participate in this toy experience. That's part of the play value of an activity toy. Sitting together, figuring out how to make the item, and then enjoying it when the item is complete is the appropriate play pattern. You're leveraging the toy to create a shared experience. Be sure to make a big deal over the finished product—that's part of the fun. Activity toy products can make great family gifts. Grandparents and other recipients will usually be wholly unconcerned with the artistic talent evident in the item and fully pleased that it was made for them.

Outdoor Toys

Go out and play! That's no longer just the cry of the busy parent. Now it's a message from the medical community. With childhood obesity on the rise in the United States, health professionals say it is more important than ever to encourage our children to engage in physical activity. And often, that means getting the children up off the couch and getting them outside. Toys can play an important role in this process. The more you have on hand that would be fun for outdoor play, the more excited the kids will be about getting outdoors and working up a sweat. If there's nothing fun to do outside, it'll only be a matter of minutes before they've gravitated back to the TV or some other sedentary activity.

Riding Toys

Some of the most popular outdoor toys are riding toys. They can be toys with mini motors or those that move only with kid power. All provide both physical and developmental benefits.

Benefits   Riding toys can enhance gross motor skills. When shared with friends or siblings, these vehicles can be platforms for teaching turn taking and sharing. They also foster fantasy play.

Timing   When a child can reliably sit up without toppling over, you can introduce some early riding toys. Often the best choice for littlest ones are push riding toys—those without additional motor power. In most cases, this is plenty fast for a baby, and you don't have to worry about the little ones outdistancing you. Riding toys that look like cars, trains, boats, or animals are all fun. Look for manufacturers you recognize—they often build the sturdiest ride-ons. Also, for additional play value, particularly in the preschool age group, look for riding toys that have additional features, such as a dirt digger, horns and bells, or carrying compartments.

Once a child can power the toy alone, the parent should stop pushing. Riding toys provide an excellent way to build motor skills, and if you're doing all the work, there's no learning going on. Trikes and wagons that come with parental handles are convenient for parents but not the best way to improve skills and serve up the benefits of exercise. Instead, leave time for a leisurely walk down the bike path or sidewalk—one that goes at the toddler's pace. Sure, you'd get there faster if you did all the pushing, but you'd be dampening a key benefit of the toy.

TOY TIP

Ride-ons are kid magnets—you'll find the neighbor children are eager to come by for a ride. But try to keep the crowd to a minimum. The benefit of the toy comes in its actual use—not in waiting in line for all the other kids to have their turn. Sharing and turn taking are most easily accomplished in small groups rather than in large crowds.

Warning   Motorized riding toys are great fun, and they're fine when properly supervised. You should be outside with the child at all times and have scanned the area for possible safety hazards. Lots of children will not be able to stop on command, so don't assume that shouting distance is close enough. Especially in the early stages of riding toy experiences, you should be close enough to catch and hold the vehicle.

Outside Toys

If it doesn't have wheels and won't be ruined by a night in a snowstorm, it's an outside toy. It can be anything from a slide to a sandbox to a picnic table. There are several important considerations when it comes to purchasing outside toys, almost all of them related to adult aesthetics, so don't feel guilty about making your feelings known when it comes to this category.

TOY TIP

Get an outdoor toy box. A sturdy, weather-resist-
ant container should have a spot outside or near
a door, and all outdoor toys should live there. If
outdoor toys constantly make the trek in and out of
the house, they're bound to track in dirt and germs.
Give them their own outdoor storage space and
wash the box and its contents on a regular basis.

Benefits Toys designed for the yard or other outdoor
setting encourage physical play, and that helps build gross
motor skills. They can encourage group play and fantasy
play.

Timing Outdoor play is fun and appropriate for all ages,
but be sure you pick an outside toy that fits with a child's
current age. It's not uncommon for a parent to consider
buying an outside toy that is somewhat ahead of a child's
current abilities, figuring he or she will "grow into it." This
may sound good financially, but safetywise it's a bad idea.
Especially in the case of climbing toys or others that re
quire certain gross motor skills, a toy that is above a child's
ability can be dangerous. Be sure you are stocking the
yard with toys that kids can safely use now.

Warning How big is your outdoor space? You'll want to
pick items that fit reasonably in the yard or other outdoor

area that you have available. An outside toy that overwhelms the outdoor space and makes it impossible for
adults to enjoy fresh air along with the kids is a mistake.
There are lots of sizes to choose from—pick one that
leaves some ground area for the grown-ups.

Colors are also important. This toy is essentially your
lawn decor. So if bright red is going to irritate you, try
some more neutral shades. Again, it's likely that you'll
have some choices, so envision yourself looking out your
kitchen window over the next five years and seeing this
object in your yard. Pick a color you can live with.

Sports Toys

Many parents are eager for their little ones to grow up and
join them in playing their favorite sports. Sports toys are
a great way to introduce the games and the early stages of
play. The choice of toy and the timing of the introduction
can help encourage your little future sports fan.

Benefits   Sports toys encourage physical activity—
something that is sorely lacking in the lives of many kids
today. By introducing sports toys to a young child, you lay
the groundwork for future participation.

Timing   Although you may want to hold off on true competitive sports until school starts, sports toys are a great
addition to the toy box, and at a very early age. As soon as
your little one can throw, buy a ball—a nice small one that
he or she can handle. When kids understand the concept
of kicking (often in the toddler years), introduce soccer
balls. Rules and competition may be more than these

TOY TIP

When the child is three or four, depending on his or her personality, you might want to introduce the more structured concept of competitive play. The game can be within your own family or in an organized league—something like a local T-ball league or soccer league may work. At this age, kids most enjoy running around outside and participating in snack time, but it's still a good introduction to the experience. Be sure even at this stage that you are a good sports parent, behaving appropriately at games and showing enthusiasm and support for your child without belittling the other team. Kids learn their sports-related behavior from their parents, and this is important role-modeling time.

preschoolers understand, but they can still get a great deal of enjoyment and benefit out of sports toys.

Early balls should be soft and easy to handle. A football is fine for a baby or toddler, so long as it's made of soft material. The same is true for soccer and basketballs. Small children will enjoy playing catch, and it's a great way to improve coordination and teach interactive play skills. If you've got a real adult sports fan in the family, you can seek out sports toys designed to look like the real thing, but hold off buying regulation equipment. It may seem cute to put a basketball in the crib, but really, baby isn't ready to get the most out of that level of toy, and it can create a safety hazard.

Warning   If you introduce your child to sports toys, be sure you are introducing your child to good sports behavior. Even when playing catch with your child or sitting together to watch a game, model the kind of behavior you hope to see your child display one day on the field. If you are bad-mouthing the other team, you can bet even your young child is listening and learning.

Conclusion

Throughout any child's life, a wide variety of toy types will come and go. There will be some years when a particular category is a runaway favorite and others when a child's taste runs to many kinds of toys. For parents, the key is to understand the full spectrum of what's available and make the right match at the right time for their own child.

WORSHEET
Toy Type Your Child

Take a short quiz to help you better understand your child's preferred toy types. Keep in mind that toy preferences can change over time, so results today may be different six months down the road.

Does your child . . .
A. Prefer to play alone?
B. Prefer to play with playmates or siblings?

A. Prefer open-ended play with no time limits on any toy or play activity?
B. Have siblings or playmates (for example, at day care) with whom to share toys?

A. Enjoy repetitive play with one kind of toy?
B. Change toys often during play?

A. Enjoy competitive play?
B. Ask constantly for new toys?

Results and Suggestions

If your answers are mostly A's, your child is an independent player. Choose toys that encourage self-challenge and individual creativity; puzzles and single-use art, craft, or science kits are good choices.

If your answers were mostly B's, your child seeks out the social stimulation of peer play. Consider activity sets and toys that encourage sharing or team play.

If your answers are a mix of both A's and B's, your child has a creative streak. Look for toys that encourage make-believe and role-playing situations.

Tales from the Toy Tips Lab

It took a room full of four-year-olds to show us how times have changed and how we as adults need to adapt. We were testing a new doll, one that came with lipstick and would leave a kiss-print on your face. The children, a mix of boys and girls, took the doll with them into their little playhouse. Later, when they emerged, not only were the boys playing with the doll, they were covered in the lipstick. Some of the parents weren't too happy to see their boys playing with dolls. But they realized, as we did, that times have evolved and boys have too. The new age of involved, attentive dads is producing a new generation of boys who see playing with dolls as just fine. The toy types that were presented to you in your childhood may not be the toy types that engage your child.

Chapter 3

Ages and Stages

No two kids are alike. That's true even among close siblings. One child will be an avid reader at age seven, the other will prefer sports or puzzles. One will spend hours acting out fantasies staffed with Barbie dolls and stuffed animals; another isn't entertained unless a game board and dice are involved. Like their adult counterparts, kids can develop a wide variety of highly individualized tastes.

Fortunately, amid this mass of picks and preferences, we can make some generalizations. The overall timeline of human development does offer some guidelines for the toy buyer that can aid in selection. Although no two children will warm to the same toy the same way, it's likely that those two learned to sit up, throw a ball, or read game directions at roughly the same age. So when you are picking a toy, it's a smart idea to start with chronological age as your first signpost. Age is by no means the final word on good toy selection, but it's an excellent beginning.

Keep in mind that what you're looking to do is make a good fit between the toy and the child's developmental level. A toy that is below a child's developmental skills will soon be discarded as boring. Then again, a toy that is too challenging may lead to frustration and a quick trip to the bottom of the toy box. What's more, research has shown that even though a developmental clock may be set by biology, the honing of key skills can be positively affected by your choice of toys. But even before you begin looking at specific toys, you have choices to make. As the adult, you are looking for a connection between a child's developmental stage and the toy. The more closely you make this match, the more fun and educational the toy will be.

The next sections describe some general guidelines for ages and stages.

Infants: Birth Through One Year

Good news! At this stage, a child's most important and treasured plaything is you. Mom and dad and other important adults are endlessly fascinating to babies. Watch them as they watch you. Your eyes, your voice, your clothes—all are high entertainment to a little one just exploring the world for the first time. Don't be afraid to be a baby toy yourself. Remember that this is part of how a baby learns to see the world and engage in early play. Play peekaboo, sing songs, read books and nursery rhymes. All too soon, you'll be competing with the wide world for the child's attention. Enjoy your time in the spotlight.

What toys should share this special stage with you? Look for items designed specifically for infants that offer baby a chance to explore new shapes, colors, and sounds. Lightweight toys, such as rattles, and squishy toys that encourage grasping and holding are good choices.

This is an age when well-chosen crib toys can be especially popular with both baby and parent. Mobiles are lovely nursery decoration and can also be great first toys, even though baby may never do more than gaze adoringly at the design. Research has suggested that infants are visually attracted to stark black-and-white designs in their first months, so even though the more colorful mobiles may seem more attractive to the adult buyer, keep your tiny recipient's tastes in mind. Some more advanced mobile designers have come up with ways to change or swap out mobile artwork. Adding color to the mobile as he or she grows can be entertaining for baby and visually pleasing to the adults of the household, too.

Be sure that the mobile you pick is designed for use in a baby's crib. (Those meant purely as artwork aren't always safe for a nursery.) It should attach securely and out of baby's reach. Also, when installing a mobile, keep in mind that adults will be entering the room and reaching for baby in the middle of the night. Position the mobile so that it doesn't poke mom in the eye when she arrives for the midnight feeding. Finally, compare design features. Some have setups that allow you to push the mobile to the side when not in use.

What about in-crib entertainment systems? Many toy companies have recently come out with fairly extensive models that offer music and visual entertainment and can be operated by the cursory swat of an infant. Two things to keep in mind when considering this type of toy: first, the bells and whistles are engaging, but they're more likely to impress adults than babies. Often, far less technically advanced toys are just as entertaining to little ones. So don't think you have to go high-tech or risk boring the baby. Second, if baby can operate the music-and-light toy on his own (as opposed to an overhead mobile that he can't reach), he'll be able to do it anytime. And that could be in the middle of the night, when you'd prefer that he roll over and go back to sleep. So crib entertainment systems can be fun, but you should weigh the pros and cons before investing.

Specially designed floor mats make excellent first toys. Babies often spend quite a bit of time on the floor, and a well-crafted mat can provide plenty of entertainment. Look for stark, contrasting colors and designs that will catch baby's eye. Many are also made with a variety of textures and securely attached elements for baby to explore. Avoid anything with pieces that can detach. They can be hazards for baby and a hassle for mom. Also, floor mats should be easy to machine wash and dry.

Once a child can sit up—often that's at about six or seven months—toy needs begin to change. More toys that require a baby to use his burgeoning holding and grasping skills can enter the picture. Blocks are a great choice now. Nesting cups and stacking rings can be endlessly interesting to a growing baby, who will delight in figuring out how these items come together, come apart, come together, come apart. It's all a fascinating process when you're just discovering toys you can control on your own.

Another hint: look for toys that encourage reaching. Again, this fits nicely with a developmental skill set. Baby can enjoy the toy and expand on her newfound skills.

A note on skill building: many parents want to do everything they can to help their little ones advance, but this is a notion that should be carefully managed when it comes to toy buying. It's fine, even preferable, to look for toys that will encourage a baby to build on naturally occurring developmental skills. But buying more advanced toys to speed the process is not advisable. A toy that is too complicated or too difficult to use will often frustrate your little one. The concept of sticking to a task and learning a difficult new skill is one that is still many years off. Babies are much more grounded in the present.

What's more, a toy designed for an older child is often unsafe in the hands of a younger baby. It may have small pieces, sharp edges, or other elements that may be perfectly safe for older kids but inappropriate for babies. So although you want to do all you can to help your baby

TOY TIP

Check out these toys and ways to play:

- *Stuffed toys.* Great for older infants (six months and up), but be sure they pass the safety test. Give a tug to the eyes, ears, and any other elements to be sure they can't come off and become a choking risk. Even better—look for plush toys that have sewn features rather than plastic ones that are glued on. Also, don't keep stuffed toys in a crib overnight. Like pillows or bedding, they can be a suffocation hazard. Keep them for daytime play.
- *Activity toys.* Excellent, so long as they are geared toward developmentally appropriate infant activities, such as stacking, reaching, and opening and closing. More complex activities, such as sorting, two-step processes, or craft toys will be more attractive later on.
- *Musical toys.* Babies love music, so offer up musical toys. Some music toys are made so that baby can operate them alone; others require an adult to work the gears. Baby will probably love the tune you find the most grating, but get used to it. If there's one thing babies love more than music, it's repetitious music. Some research argues that classical music is more developmentally beneficial to babies than more simple nursery tunes. But it's actually not the sophistication of the music that attracts baby—it's the

> rhythm. So rhythmic music of all kinds, be it full orchestral symphonies or African drums, is likely to produce benefits.

advance along the developmental curve, be sure that any toy you buy for a baby meets infant safety standards—no small parts or detachable fabric or plastic pieces. Children this age will often try to explore new objects by popping them into their mouths, and that's a choking hazard.

Toddlers: One to Three Years

If only you could bottle the boundless energy of a toddler. Having fully mastered the art of walking, a toddler seems in constant motion. Running, reaching, crawling, climbing. Sit still? What's that?

Best advice? Go with it. Toys that get a toddler running and walking and working on those already developing motor skills are important. They not only help build muscle groups and balance but also keep your little one interested in something other than leaping off your sofa or scaling the bookcases.

Sitting quietly, coloring or working on a fine motor task, isn't completely out of the question at this age. But it will be out of the ordinary. So look for toys that dovetail with a toddler's physical activity level. For indoor play, look for chunky blocks, large-piece puzzles, and other toys with a truly physical bent. Pick items that can take a lot of punishment so that when the user decides to step on it, throw it, or drop it from the top of the staircase, the toy will survive the abuse. Avoid toys that are delicate or require careful setup or assembly. Toddlers don't know their own strength, and a less-than-sturdy toy doesn't stand a chance.

For children this age, it's a great idea to introduce board books. Certainly, you can read to a child from a traditional book, but board books offer the child a chance to have some hands-on experience in prereading. Look for bright colors, nursery rhymes, and lots of pictures. Even very basic texts, with photographs and shapes, can be very popular, and they help foster the notion of reading as a fun activity. Sit and read with your child or let the toddler sit and turn pages independently. Both are good play activities and help build an appreciation for reading that will come in handy down the road.

Bath toys are also a good category at this age. Toddlers often love the splashing and close parental attention of bath time. Look for toys that interact with the water— toys that pour, float, squirt, or blow bubbles are good choices. Intricate setups of pirate ships or mermaid scenes can be fun, but they're not necessary for engaged water play. Be sure the toys you pick can handle prolonged water exposure. Some plastic toys may look bath safe but fall apart or attract mildew. Keep this in mind as well for any kitchen containers, such as Tupperware, that you might want to draft into bathtub duty. Toys specifically designed for bath use are often a smart choice for long-lasting water fun. Remember to give the bath toys a good scrubbing on a regular basis. Put them through the dishwasher (top rack) or hand wash with warm soapy water.

Some basic bath tools can double as toys. Washcloths in puppet shapes are fun; so are animal-shaped sponges. If you're going to pick toylike soaps or cleansing products, take special care to buy recognized brand names. Not all kids' soap is created equal. Some fun-looking items like soap crayons or bubble baths may be hard to clean from the tub surface or even irritating to toddler skin. So be sure to pick a quality manufacturer with a history of producing appropriate bath products for kids. If you notice any skin irritation, consider any bubble baths or specialty soaps prime suspects. Even well-made products can be hard on some types of young skin. If your child has allergies, check with your pediatrician on any new skin products.

Whatever your choice of bath toy, the most important element is adult supervision. Never ever walk away from a toddler in the bathtub. Although he may seem perfectly secure and confident sitting in the tub, he can still drown in even a small amount of water if left unattended. Don't leave the bathroom when your toddler is in the water. And if you must leave, grab a towel and take your little one with you.

For outdoor play, look for toys that promote a range of motion. Ride-ons—with big, safe wheels and a limited speed—are great fun. Be sure that the vehicle isn't swift enough to get away from an adult arm's length. Some forward-thinking manufacturers of tricycles have come up with an edition that includes an adult control bar, so your little one can pedal away but you can hang on securely. Ride-on cars, trucks, wagons, and other vehicles—all powered solely by little feet—are good picks. Seek out safe ride-on locations. Driveways are smooth and flat, but they lead to the street and are often not the best place for a toddler on wheels. Consider parks and playgrounds with paved sections as best bets. Bike paths, if not too well traveled by adult athletes, are also a good location.

Ball play is big fun for toddlers. Look for a combination of sizes and textures. Actual sports equipment, such

TOY TIP

Check out these toys and ways to play:

- **Riding toys.** Great for working off excess toddler energy. Look for vehicles that are toddler powered (no additional power source). Consider ride-ons with adult control attachments if you'll be cruising the neighborhood near older kids or adults on wheels.
- **Outdoor toys.** Sandbox toys, balls, and other fresh-air favorites are a good pick at this age. Keep in mind that toddlers often throw toys with a certain amount of abandon, especially outside, so be mindful of the objects you place in their hands.
- **Puzzles.** Oh, for a small sliver of quiet time. Puzzles can help. Look for big, chunky pieces and easy designs. Licensed characters are a great addition to this play category, thanks to the large selection of recognizable characters. Puzzles made of sturdy plastic or wood will hold up better than those made from cardboard or other paper substance. Foam-based puzzles are also a fine choice, though some may be too delicate for the playful toddler fist.

as footballs or basketballs, may be problematic. Because they are designed for a much larger user, they're heavy for a toddler and more likely to result in a painful bounce encounter. A toddler with any regulation sports equipment requires close supervision so that no one gets hurt. You're better off picking a toddler-friendly ball—made of foam or other soft-textured material—with a true-to-life sports design. The little ones will be just as impressed if the basketball looks like a basketball but doesn't hurt their toes when it bounces.

In addition to being in constant motion, children in this age group very much like to imitate their elders. Kitchens, workshops, grocery stores, and baby-care stations are likely to be familiar backdrops to scenarios that toddlers will enjoy re-enacting. As with ride-ons, look for sturdiness of construction as well as fun play elements, such as storage spots and things that make noise. Feel free to add your own elements to the play scheme. If your toddler likes playing kitchen, you can offer up some plastic storage containers or sippy cups to be part of the set. An extra washcloth or baby blanket can be part of a baby-care setup. Watch the toddler play and see what makes a natural addition.

A wise parent will stock up on toys such as play telephones, laundry sets, and cooking toys. Without play versions of these enticing adult items, your child is likely to try to play with the real thing. That can be a problem when you're looking for your cell phone or car keys and realize you last saw them in the hands of your two-year-old. As was the case with infants, be sure any toy you purchase meets safety standards for the age group. Under-threes may still put interesting objects in their mouths. Don't be tempted to give your toddler the cast-off TV remote or some other consumer electronics item. They're not designed for toddlers and are not safe as toys.

Preschool: Three to Five Years

Welcome to the land of make-believe. This is the magical time in a child's life when anything is possible. Elephants have wings and land in the backyard. Monsters hide in the closet and must be strictly shooed away at bedtime. Ariel the Mermaid just came into the kitchen and announced that nobody has to eat broccoli. The line between fact and fiction is decidedly blurry for the preschooler. These newly minted imaginations are out for their first spins, and it's all the adults can do to keep up.

At this age, children begin to truly explore the thrill of pretend play. They'll need little in the way of props, but there's plenty you can add to the mix to promote fun and learning. This is an age when a wide variety of "classic" toys will be well received. A traditional dollhouse stocked with doll-size family members and furniture will get hours of play. Resist the urge to choose a fancy or delicate abode. It may be lovely, but can it stand up to the punishment of an eager three-year-old? Go for solid construction. Other good choices: toy garage or railroad sets, pretend zoos or playgrounds, even make-believe schools. All will give preschoolers the chance to act out both realistic and fantastical situations. Don't be too concerned if the play pattern doesn't seem to fit the toy's "official" purpose—for example, if the kids play school with the plastic supermarket food. It's their fantasy. Join in and let their imaginations lead the way.

Dress-up clothes are also a popular choice for this age group. You can offer items from your own wardrobe as well as store-bought costumes. Be aware that dress-up is a contact sport for preschoolers, so clothes with lace or sequins or other delicate decoration may be in peril. Be sure to include accessories—hats, shoes, purses, briefcases, and so on—to help flesh out the fantasy. Be aware that at this age it is completely normal for boys and girls to try on clothes and fantasy roles of the opposite sex. It's indicative of nothing more than appropriate imaginative play.

Along these same lines of budding creativity, preschool is a wonderful time to stock up on additional art and musical toys. In art supplies, look for a variety of colors, textures, and media. Always purchase paints and other products designed for children. Those for adults may not be nontoxic. Choose tools designed for kids as well, such as low-slung easels and easy-grip paint brushes. Also, be willing to draft into art duty some common household items, such as sponges and cut potatoes. They're as much fun as any high-end art set. Above all, prepare to get messy. Nothing dampens the enthusiasm of a young artist quicker than an order to stay neat and clean. Bah. Let the art flow.

There are many great musical toys designed for this age group—everything from drum sets to battery-powered pianos. Be sure the musical toy you pick can be operated in a fun and varied way by little hands. (One-note toys will be quickly discarded as dull.) Also, consider musical toys that encourage children to make their own music as well as imitate the melodies they hear around them. For example, a toy piano that can both play popular nursery tunes and act as a free-form keyboard may fit the bill. As

TOY TIP

Check out these toys and ways to play:

- **Construction toys.** Building, banging, knocking down. All are great fun for the preschooler. Early building-block sets designed for smaller hands make great picks now.
- **Creative toys.** Toys that encourage a child to create—be it art or music or in some other medium—are a good choice now. Preschoolers are discovering the expanse of their imaginations, and they'll gladly pick up new tools of the imaginative trade.
- **Role-play toys.** Dress-up kits—everything from princess to doctor to construction worker—will help preschoolers in their urge to act out the adult roles they see around them. Look for costumes they can get in and out of easily.

with art, be prepared for exuberance to be the mood of the play moment. This is not the time in a child's life when she will entertain you with soothing evening music.

School Age: Five to Nine Years

This is a fork in the road of many a family's toy-buying journey. At this stage of toy buying, the goals of the adult and child diverge. For adults, the most important elements of toys and play at this age are educational development and the building of social skills. For kids, it's being cool and "in" with one's peers. It's also a time when media pressures, such as advertising, movie tie-ins, and television programs, will start to exert their heavy influence on children's toy cravings. Kids that were once blissfully happy in a room full of classic wooden toys may now start to clamor for the most commercialized, short-lived plastic characters any adult could imagine. But don't worry: with a little intelligent research, you can bring the parties together.

Despite the media controversy, electronic toys can be a very good pick for this age group. In fact, some recent research suggests that appropriate play with electronic toys, such as computer and video games, can be helpful in building eye-hand coordination. The key, of course, is to pick the right electronic toys and, if you are the parent, to manage them properly in the child's playtime.

When picking an electronic game, look for those that promote such skills as counting and problem solving. They needn't be "classroom-esque" to be educational. Many games engage kids in mysteries and quests and can both entertain and educate. But picking these games off the shelf is tough. It's hard to tell from the packaging what's a good game and what's a waste of money. Do some research before you head for the toy store so that you won't be swayed by the package graphics or the uniformed sales clerk. Books on electronic games are a fine resource, but keep in mind that the world of electronics is in constant flux, so recommendations about specific titles and game lines may be out-of-date. Check the publication date of any electronics game reference book. Often a website will have the most recent information.

A word on video game violence: although there has been quite a bit of government and industry discussion surrounding the issue of game violence, your role as the adult toy buyer is still the most crucial element in the mix. Don't let a rating on a box decide whether or not a particular game is appropriate for the child in your life. That is your job. Play the game yourself, if you can, to see what kind of issues are encountered by the characters. Read reviews of the product that address these issues specifically. If you have friends or know other parents with values similar to your own, ask what they've seen and what they think of a particular toy or game. The presence of combat or theft or other intense situations is not necessarily a deal breaker—you may decide that the depiction is in line with your own values and appropriate. Although you may decide not to reject the game on the basis of its violence, you will want to discuss the issue with your child to make sure he knows the real-world rules about such things as kicking and punching. And your decision to accept the game should be based on direct contact with it, not by your relying solely on the text on the back of the package. That text is designed to sell the game or toy, not to educate you or protect your child. When buying an electronic game for another person's child, it is appropriate to call in advance and ask about the family rules regarding these games.

What to do about licensed products? This is the age when the drumbeat begins. Hollywood has carefully crafted a business plan to promote its big- and small-screen entertainment by linking it to kids' toys. That means every new kids' movie, every new cartoon, every new entertainment product aimed at kids is going to come with an extensive and incessantly promoted toy line. Some of the items will be quick hits—such as action figures associated with a summer movie. Others will be far more elaborate programs, such as toys, games, and other merchandise themed to an ongoing cartoon series. Unless the child in your life is in a media-free bubble, he or she will almost certainly be exposed to these pitches. And don't blame the kids when they want the stuff. They're on the receiving end of a sophisticated marketing scheme.

What should you do? It's unwise to drop a complete ban on licensed merchandise. Like many hard-and-fast measures, it only serves to heighten the demand. The more you say no, the more kids will think it's the most desirable plaything on earth. So find your happy medium. What kinds of toys can you live with, and what kinds will you just resist? Don't be afraid to explain your thinking to your child. If you're fine with a few character items but have no intention of purchasing the entire line, make that clear. An older child may be able to look at the offerings and make choices. If you are willing to buy a licensed toy so long as it is educational, try to help your child understand the difference. Also, look at a licensed line before you say no. There may be items you can tolerate. For example, if you don't want your child to have the latest handheld video game, you might be more comfortable with the cards or coloring books that feature the characters. These can allow your child to participate in the social aspects of the entertainment trend without your bending your toy rules.

This is also a key time to discuss commercials with your kids. Although you can't expect them to be truly savvy consumers, it's appropriate to explain to them what commercials are and what they're trying to accomplish. Marketing is a very powerful force. Adults are certainly swayed by it—we have a nation full of consumers eating hamburgers and driving SUVs to prove it. So address the issue with the child in your life. You might say, "The person who made this commercial is trying to convince you

TOY TIP

Check out these toys and ways to play:

- **Action figures.** These are especially popular with boys, but many lines are hot with girls as well. They may be classic comic book heroes you recognize or a new breed of superhero. Ask about the characters and try to learn their stories. Also, keep in mind that passions for particular characters may be fleeting. If you're buying the toy as a gift, you might want to check and see if the character is still in favor.

- **Outdoor toys.** Don't forget sports as a great source of play at this age. For many children, it will be the first time they encounter group or team play. Soccer balls, T-ball sets, and other items designed for this age group will encourage them to try these activities. Don't buy sports equipment designed for adults or teens. It may be frustrating or even dangerous for a little one to use.

- **Board games.** By this age, children have learned the concept of turn taking, which means that board games can be a great toy category. Look for games with clear, relatively simple rules. Classic games can make for fun family time.

to buy this game, but you don't have to. You don't have to buy everything you see on TV. In this family, we don't run out and buy everything we see on TV." Don't expect overnight buy-in to your media plan, but keep it up. Over the course of their development, kids must learn to evaluate the marketing messages they see and hear. By talking with them now, you're laying the groundwork for a lifelong consumer education.

Preteen: Nine to Twelve Years

Kids are oh-so-cool at this age, but guess what? They'll still play with toys. Toy makers certainly haven't given up on this age group, in recent years creating and promoting a host of new toys designed with preteens in mind. The adult toy buyer may not be familiar with the toy companies targeting this age group, so a good bit of research goes a long way in making a good choice.

Consider strategy games. These are a bit higher up the intellectual food chain from traditional board games and can be great for fostering thinking skills and providing entertaining social play. Some basics you'll remember: checkers, for example, is an excellent choice for this age group. Newer game titles that allow the players to discover a treasure, unravel a mystery, or otherwise plot and scheme to win are good picks. Group games are also fun. Kid versions of popular adult games and other activity games are available and can be a great way to foster family game time.

Handheld and video games are also extremely popular with this age group. As with younger kids, the key to purchasing in this category is to have knowledge of the games and reasonable family rules surrounding play. Many

TOY TIP

Check out these toys and ways to play:

- **Sports toys.** At this age, more traditional sports equipment may be appropriate. Be sure you have some familiarity with the child's skill level before you buy.
- **Board games.** Children this age are a long way from the kiddie games, but strategy, mystery, or group activity board games can be great fun and good builders of social skills.
- **Construction toys.** Plastic building blocks? Nah. Think complicated building sets, complete with robotics and moving parts. They can be challenging and fun and far from the brightly colored toys of early childhood.

of the electronic games have advanced in sophistication so that they allow team play and other social activities. Understand what the child wants to do with the game and observe the child in play. Is the electronic game a source of isolation, keeping the child from other activities? If so, you may want to try to introduce some new interests. But if the game is a source of social contact and discussion, it can be part of a positive social experience and therefore simply requires appropriate monitoring.

Kids this age may want to play Internet games, and this is a good age to lay down "cyber-rules": strictly enforce your rules regarding email or instant message contact online. Visit the Internet sites your child plays, and play the games to see what she is seeing. If possible, have your child use a computer that is in a public family area, such as a den or family room, rather than an office or bedroom where you can't monitor her activity as closely. Ask, read, and surf. The Internet is a fertile playground for kids, and you need to know what's out there.

Conclusion

Nothing about childhood is carved in stone. Every child will move through these early years on his or her own timetable, acquiring skills, tastes, and toys on a personally programmed schedule. Your role as the parent is to understand the basic parameters of age and stage and make choices that offer children appropriate toys at appropriate age windows. It's more art than science, but there's no one better than you to make the call.

WORKSHEET

Doing and Playing

This worksheet is an idea chart designed as a way for
parents to keep track as a child acquires a skill and then
to choose toys that are age appropriate and will continue
to enhance that skill. Remember, all children develop at
their own pace.

Skills	Toys
Infant	
Listening	Rattles, books, music
Focusing on objects and swatting	Mobiles, crib and floor activity gyms
Grasping, reaching	Nesting blocks
Pulling head up	Tummy toys
Pressing	Books with sound
Holding, hugging	Stuffed toys, dolls
Pulling up, balancing	Push toys, pull toys
Mouthing	Teethers
Sitting	Bath and sand toys, stuffed toys
Standing	Push-behind toys
Walking	Pull-along toys
Blowing	Bubbles
Manipulating objects	Shape sorters
Toddler	
Developing fine motor skills	Ball drops, abacus, pop-up books, crayons, finger paints, large construction blocks, modeling dough, puppets

Engaging in pretend play, imitation	Tool kit, doctor sets, kitchen sets, dolls, costumes, telephone
Developing gross motor skills	Large balls, climbing structures, slides, foam mats, ride-ons, wagons
Understanding patterns and rhythms	Puzzles, musical instruments, memory and matching games, phonics, alphabet toys
Understanding spatial relationships	Remote-control toys, activity playsets, water toys

Preschool

Following rules	Age-appropriate board games, sports toys
Sharing	Construction toys, activity sets, outdoor climbers
Preparing for school	Spelling, math toys, read-along books

School Age

Developing concentration	Trivia games, magic sets
Strategic thinking	Challenging board games, brain teasers, science activity kits
Promoting educational reinforcement	Math, spelling, history, and geography toys
Fostering individual creativity	Craft kits, advanced construction sets, art, karaoke, microscopes

Tales from the Toy Tips Lab

There's hardly a parent on the planet that doesn't think his or her offspring is a genius, so I was not surprised during one toy test when a father approached me and said that his four-year-old son wanted to test out the construction set meant for an older child. With his father supervising but not directing, the boy soon was constructing a robot as tall as he was, complete with detailed features and working parts. Some children learn more quickly than others. However, there is no reason to push a child to excel faster than his or her abilities dictate. If you find yourself in this situation, be sure that safety is your first concern. Then remember to interact with your child and have some fun.

Chapter 4

Special Situations

No two children will learn and develop at the same pace. And even given these expected differences, you may find situations that require special attention. Whether it's a particular strength or weakness or family circumstance that sets them apart, there are children whose needs are specific and distinct. These special situations call for special consideration in a host of activities, including the purchasing of toys.

When you have a child in your life who is different from the majority in some way, don't pretend there's no difference at all. In many cases, the child already knows there's something that makes him or her unique. Certainly, you as the adult know and are required to make appropriate choices based on your knowledge. Pretending somehow that the special circumstance, whatever it is, does not exist does the child a disservice. If you don't understand how best to buy a toy for a child in an unusual circumstance, educate yourself.

Special situations come in all shapes and sizes. What follows is a discussion of some of the most common.

Special Needs

In previous generations, a disability meant a physical challenge; today, special needs run a much wider gamut. You might find a child who struggles with communication, a child who is delayed in the acquisition of some motor skills, or a child with attention deficit issues. These, alongside the more commonly recognized issues of vision or hearing impairment or other more visible physical challenges, make up the much diversified world of disability today. Just as the types of disability are quite varied, so too are the degrees of severity. You will find children who are clearly different to the untrained eye and others for whom a disability is masked to all but a parent or experienced therapist.

A child with special needs, whatever they may be, is a child with special toy needs as well. Properly chosen toys can be true tools that aid a child in addressing his or her difficulties. At the same time, however, toys chosen without consideration of a child's special issues may lead to frustration. The most important thing you can do, as a parent buying for your own child or someone else's, is to understand as much as you can about the nature of the child's special needs and get advice as to what type of toy to buy.

Toy Types and Their Special Needs Applications

Some toys lend themselves particularly well to specific special needs. Although there are no hard-and-fast rules as to how toys can be adapted for a child with special needs, some categories are well suited to the task and are often used by therapists and teachers to help children with challenges master classroom and general life skills. You may want to experiment with a variety of toy types to see which ones bring out the best in your child. Here are some categories to start with:

- *Board games.* These are excellent for children with difficulty mastering social or communications skills. A well-designed board game with age-appropriate rules and clear objectives can be very useful in helping a child master such tasks as turn taking and interaction with peers. Board games provide a structured play environment in which there are rules, objectives, and winners and losers. Playing within such a structure allows a child to exercise fledgling social skills. Choose a game that is appropriate to the age of the child: a young child who is still a prereader might enjoy one that is highly visual; an older child might be more ready for a complicated strategy game. Parents may want to play with their child, to model the appropriate social and communication behaviors expected during the game.

- ***Electronic games.*** In some cases, computer or other tech-related toys can be beneficial in building attention skills. A child with difficulties in this area may be better engaged by the technological aspects of the toy. Some well-designed computer games reward attention by adding difficulty as the child progresses successfully through the game. Not all technology toys are alike, so do some research before making a purchase. Choosing a game that reflects a child's interests, such as sports or animals, will help make the initial match between game and child. Play the game yourself first so that you are familiar enough with it to provide support and guidance. That's also a good way to screen for inappropriate content. Sometimes games contain scenes that you may not find appropriate for your child. Also be aware that some children with special needs are highly sensitive to sound. Toys should have easily manipulated volume control.

- ***Sports toys.*** Some well-meaning adults often decline to buy an uncoordinated child a sports-related toy, thinking it would somehow be unfair to give the child such an item. In fact, a child working to catch up in gross motor skills can often benefit from a sports toy, provided it is well chosen. Softer foam balls can give a child a chance to practice the art of throwing and catching without getting hurt. Toss games that include Velcro mitts and other assistive technology can be fun and good for practice. Just because a child isn't yet at the same level as her peers in sports doesn't mean she will never attain that goal. Well-chosen sports toys, designed to help build skills rather than highlight weaknesses, can help. Play with your child and be positive about his performance.

- *Fantasy toys.* A great way to help a child with special needs through play is by engaging his or her imagination. Fantasy toys—everything from puppets to dress-up clothes—can be used creatively. Fantasy play can provide avenues for communication, experience in the social skill of pretending with peers, and a window of insight for a parent who might want to know better what a child is thinking and feeling.

- *Noisy toys.* Toys that have volume are useful in many situations. For a child who is visually impaired, a toy that uses sound may be great fun because it plays to the child's strength. A hearing-impaired child may even use a toy with sound—provided it has enough volume. Keep in mind that toys that are too loud defeat their own purpose. Look for a volume control knob—one that both you and the child can operate.

Accommodations

Once you've chosen your toys, be prepared to adapt them to the needs of the child. There are many ways to make a toy fit a child's special needs. Be creative in your approach.

Just because everyone else isn't playing with the toy in that way doesn't mean you can't make up your own approach. Most good toys can be played with in a variety of ways.

How can you customize a toy experience?

First, consider the setting. Where you play can have a direct impact on the child's ability to enjoy the toy and the playtime. Be creative in your setup. A child with difficulty attending may have better concentration sitting in a chair at a table rather than on the floor of the living room. A child working on sensory-processing issues may be more comfortable indoors than out. A child with low vision will need more sustained lighting, and a child with hearing difficulties may do better in a room without background noise. Children are often not yet mature enough to make their own environmental demands known. Scan your play area with the child's special needs in mind before sitting down to play. That may help lead to a more fulfilling experience.

You may also consider adapting the rules to the child's unique situation. After all, just because a toy or game comes with rules doesn't mean you're bound by their dictates. Sure, learning to play by the rules is part of life and growing up. But sometimes it is appropriate to adapt the rules so that the toy or game can produce the most fun and learning. Major League Baseball says three strikes and you're out, but there's no reason your game can't go to ten strikes and take a base. Who's looking? All games are adaptable. Rules that you may consider adapting include number of turns, time limits, even rules for winners and losers. All rules can be bent if fun is on the line.

Warning: when you want to bend the rules to your own play experience, that's fine. But in some cases, it is wise to articulate to the child that you are making these adaptations. Consider that the child may encounter this same toy or game in a different setting—say, at a friend's house or therapist's office. It may frustrate or confuse the child if he or she thinks this new person is playing the game "wrong." Be clear that you are initiating changes or adaptations to the toy or game; that way the child won't be surprised to see others follow a different set of rules.

Another popular way to adapt a toy or game is to play with partners or in teams. If a child has trouble either with managing the physical aspects of play, such as the motor coordination involved, or with following the rules or maintaining appropriate social interaction, it can make sense to partner the child with a more secure player. That other player can be another child, a parent, or a teacher. This way, the child can participate in the playtime with some support. That kind of supportive experience can eventually lead to the child's being able to manage the play experience solo.

Where to Get Advice

The most important aspect of buying a toy for a child with special needs is to know as much as you possibly can about the individual child. All children are different, and a child with a special need is no exception. Look for specific advice if you can—before going to the toy store. Who should you ask?

- *Parents.* They are the key authorities on the needs and toy desires of their children. Don't be afraid to ask for fear of insulting the parent or seeming critical of the child. It is not impolite to be sensitive to a child with special needs. Many parents would prefer that their friends and relatives confront the issue of a child's special needs in an up-front and clear way, rather than attempt to sweep the issue under the rug. When you seek advice from a parent of a child with special needs, be positive in your approach. Say, "I'd like to buy a toy [he or she] will really like and play with. Can you give me any tips?" Most parents will be happy to share advice and suggestions. And there may be many issues that you aren't aware of, such as a child's sensitivity to noise or a parent's desire to help the child work on a particular skill.

- *Teachers.* A child's teacher is a great source of information. The teacher sees the child in action every day and may have great suggestions as to the ways that play and toys can be beneficial. Often teachers are quite savvy about how to leverage play for acquiring classroom skills. Some teachers can recommend specific toys. Others will be able to articulate what kinds of skills the child needs to build, and you may be able to match those needs with a particular toy.

- *Therapists.* A parent may want to ask his or her child's therapists about toy suggestions. Therapists are often plugged in to new and creative ways to leverage play and toys to teach a child with special needs. Also, there are a number of retailers and catalogues that sell specially to the therapist community. The average consumer may not come across these merchants in everyday shopping. So it pays to ask the therapist—he or she may have excellent suggestions and mail-order retailers to recommend. Warning: a good therapist should not discuss his or her clients with anyone other than the parents. So if you're looking for advice and you are not the parent of the child, don't be put off if the therapist can't speak to you in specifics. It would be unethical for the therapist to share information about the child with outside individuals.

TOY TIP

It's not uncommon for a child with special needs to resist new toys. Also, some children with attention deficit issues will flit from toy to toy, limiting the amount of value and fun they can pull from any one item. One way to combat these difficulties is to set up the play area with an "all done" bin. Here's how it works: a child plays with a toy. When he puts the toy down, it goes into the "all done" bin and can't be selected again until the next play session. This encourages the child to play with toys for a greater length of time in a sitting and also helps him broaden his available selection of playthings.

- *Online communities.* Many parents, therapists, and other interested parties congregate in online communities to discuss issues and trade advice. The Internet is vast and diverse, and chances are good that whatever special need you are confronting, there is a group online discussing it right now. These virtual discussions take many forms. They may be public bulletin boards, private online communities open only to members, email newsletters, or email discussion groups. You can find the format that works for you. This is often a good way to stay on top of the latest news about new therapies or even great new toys. Warning: be careful about sharing personal details online. Although you may want to discuss your situation specifically with like-minded individuals, be judicious about sharing such information as your last name, hometown, or phone number. Not everyone online is who he or she appears to be, and it's wise to be cautious.

Twins and Multiples

Time was when twins were a rarity. But today, twins and even triplets are not uncommon. Increased use of fertility drugs and in vitro fertilization has fueled the trend. So the likelihood that a family will have twins or multiples as relatives or friends is much higher, which means more families will have to learn these children's special toy needs. It's not as simple as buying two of everything. Twins' and multiples' needs vary depending on their age and stage.

- *Babies.* Early on, you might consider buying similar but not identical toys for twins. So if you're buying plush, get a giraffe and a monkey; if it's going to be vehicles, buy a car and a truck. Do buy two toys. There's almost no hope that an infant will be able to share, even with his or her biologically closest relative. The concept is still some years away. Encourage relatives and friends to follow this trend. It will help them begin to see the children as distinct if they do not grow used to buying identical items.
- *Toddlers.* For some sets of twins, toddlerhood is the one time when it pays to be sure you are offering two identical toys in many situations. The competition among toddler multiples can be fierce, and often what one has, the other must have as well. You may see the logic in offering similar but not exactly the same toys. But to the toddler mind, there's no room for flexibility. If my twin has one, I must have the same thing. Period. Remem-

ber, these are toddlers, and they are rarely open to nuanced discussions. Buy two and wait for maturity to take hold. Another route: consider toys that naturally lend themselves to two or more players. Some possibilities include ride-on toys with two seats, a large playhouse big enough for more than one, or construction sets with a large selection of pieces in a variety of shapes and colors.

- *Preschoolers.* At this age, individual personalities will have begun to emerge in earnest. Take these cues to heart in your toy buying. If the twins truly do have the same interest in a particular toy category, that's fine. But as you start to see the differences—one child has a passion for puzzles and another likes to draw—foster that individuality through your toy picks. Basic board games can be introduced at this age; they often work well for families with twins or multiples. Also, look for toys that can be played by one or more—for example, ride-on toys that can have more than one passenger and electronic games that can be played alone or with a partner.

- *School age.* At this point you have two (or more) children with the same birthday, but other than that, you have distinct individuals. Be sure that your toy buying reflects their interests and desires. A school-age child will chafe at being lumped together with a twin or another sibling of a different age. Respect the fact that even though twins and triplets may arrive in the world together, they each travel separate paths: the older they get, the more individual they will become. But even while you are encouraging individuality, be mindful of the fact that toys can help build connections between rival siblings. Consider board games, more complicated

TOY TIP

With any siblings, but most particularly with twins or multiples, it is often incumbent upon the adult to set clear and defined rules. Doing so can help cut down on the fighting over toys, turns, and other playtime bonuses. So, for example, you may want to introduce an egg timer or hourglass and make this rule: you may have the toy for x amount of time, and when that time is up, you must hand it to your sibling. Another sibling harmony trick is called "First Turn." It works like this: decide by day whose turn it is to go first. If it's Monday, one child holds the privilege of first turn. On Tuesday, the next child gets the advantage. And so on. Children get used to the routine, and this kind of organization helps cut down on the competition and whining.

construction sets, and other toys that build social interaction. Creating a distinct personality is important to any child, but so is bonding with his or her sibling. Toys can help build common interests.

Where to Get Advice

As the number of multiple births has grown in recent years, so has the community of parents and professionals willing to share advice and experiences. Online communities are often a great source of information and advice. Many are not only geared to families with multiples but also arranged by age so you can meet and connect with families in similar stages. Another possibility: a multiples playgroup. Ask your pediatrician or local day-care director if there are any in your neighborhood. Or consider forming your own. Families can learn a great deal from one another.

Gifted

There are times when the term *gifted* is somewhat misleading. After all, to be considered gifted is to be considered endowed with something special and desirable. But although giftedness certainly affords a child many advantages, it can also make life more complicated. That's certainly true when it comes to toys. When you're buying toys for a gifted child, it is wise to consider the special needs and interests that the child may bring to playtime. Toys that are too easy will be tossed aside as boring, but toys designed for much older children can present their own problems. In fact, gifted children may find themselves in a peculiar kind of Twilight Zone when it comes to toys: too advanced for the toys designed for their age group, yet not quite ready to enjoy the playthings designed for more mature kids. That means a toy buyer must take special care to buy toys that fit the gifted child's special needs. Here are some suggestions:

- ***Toys that promote social connections with peers.*** Often the curse of the gifted child is that she is set apart from her peers by academic skills. That can make it harder for the child to make friends. Class work, a common task that unites most kids, doesn't work the same magic for the gifted child. So consider toy purchases that will help your child bond with peers. You may want to consider items that are associated with current popular culture. That will help the gifted child develop interests he can share with friends.

- ***Toys that branch out from educational themes.***
  Even smart children like to play. Just because a child is good at educational games—and may even enjoy them enormously—doesn't mean he or she won't get similar joy out of pure play toys that have little academic value. Toys often teach skills that are not academic. By encouraging the child to try toys outside the academic circle, you may actually help him or her develop new social and play skills.

- ***Toys that meet the child's skill level.*** This may mean aiming higher in the area in which the child is advanced—say, an academic-based game. But don't assume that a strength in one aspect of a child's life means he is advanced in everything. A child with an extraordinary memory may be spot-on age-level at other things, such as fine motor skills. A gifted artist may be far ahead of her peers in fine motor skills, but not in gross motor skills. One of the biggest mistakes parents make when buying toys is to buy "up" a skill level. Your child may indeed be destined for a Ph.D., but that doesn't mean he will enjoy a construction set meant for an older child. Not all skills develop at the same rate. Know the areas in which your child is gifted and those in which she is on the same level as her peers.

Where to Get Advice

Talking to a gifted child's teacher is a logical first step for advice. But that's not your only option. Other people to ask include parents of other gifted children, your local librarian, or a school counselor. All may be able to offer ad-

TOY TIP

Resist the urge to push your child into even more success. It's thrilling to see a child do well at something, be it academics or sports or art. But too much adult prodding can take all the joy out of the activity. And you risk turning the child away from a pursuit in which he or she is naturally talented. Also, some children respond poorly to the realization that the adults around them have developed expectations. They may worry about disappointing a parent or other adult and may withdraw from the activity to avoid potential failure, even when it's clear that the child's skills are significant. So encourage your child, but be aware of your own hopes and dreams and keep them under control. Behind many an unhappy child there is a pushy parent.

vice that is not just academic in nature but also speaks to the social and emotional aspects of child development.

Conclusion

Sometimes life throws you a curve ball. You may find yourself in a situation that requires more knowledge, more preparation, and more research than you ever anticipated. But the key is to reach out for that role and make it your own. The better educated you are about the special needs of your child—be they emotional, medical, or educational—the better are your child's chances of experiencing the joys and learning of playtime.

WORKSHEET

Play Milestones

Sometimes you may ask yourself, "Is my child's development on track?" It can be hard for you to tell. And comparisons to siblings or playmates are not reliable gauges. Every child develops at his or her own pace, so you shouldn't be too wedded to a strict developmental calendar. That said, experts have set general guidelines for the reaching of certain play skill milestones. If you are concerned at all about your child's development, trust your instincts and consult your child's doctor for specific advice.

Age	Play Skills
0–6 months	Listening, focusing on objects, swatting, reaching
6–12 months	Sitting, pulling up, standing, hugging, holding
Toddler (1–3)	Walking, transferring objects hand to hand, pretend play
Preschool (3–5)	Following rules, exhibiting memory skills, sharing
School age (5+)	Strategic thinking, concentration, teamwork

Tales from the Toy Tips Lab

Growing up with twin younger brothers, I was able to see firsthand the joys and challenges of toy buying for twins. One story comes from the Christmas when my brothers were four. Eager to help them establish their individuality, my parents had purchased different toys for each boy. Problem was, both my brothers were very interested in their car collections. So when Joe saw Jim unwrap a brand-new car carrier, he was furious. He clocked Jim over the head with his gift to demonstrate his displeasure. Fortunately, my brothers agreed to share the prized car carrier, but it was a good lesson. Although twins are individuals, they may sometimes share the same interest. In some cases, it's fine to buy identical gifts.

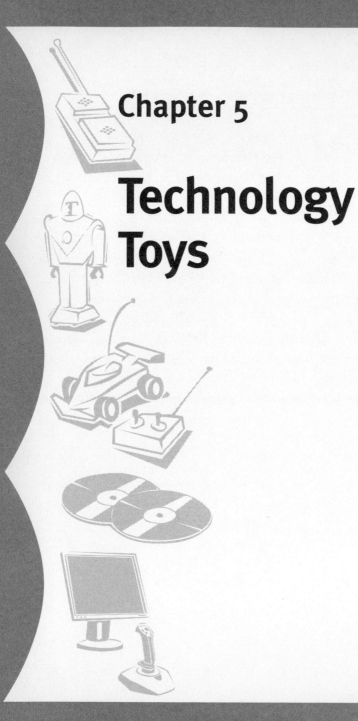

Chapter 5

Technology Toys

Technology toys have an air of mystery to them. They are quite different from what most of us experienced as children. Technology brings toys to life in ways that we only imagined as children ourselves. Toys that talk, respond, and even change and evolve with us as we learn—they're far from the playthings we remember.

With that mystery comes a host of misconceptions. Many parents are guilty of assuming that a technology toy must certainly be educational, if only by virtue of the education it took to build it. Then there are the many parents who reject tech toys as symbols of the technology army that has invaded our lives and interfered with our human relationships. Both views are too extreme. In fact, technology-enhanced toys, from computer games to interactive teddy bears, have much to offer when properly chosen and introduced to your child. The key is to understand what technology can and can't do—and, more important, what you want it to do for your child.

What Are Technology Toys?

Let's start with the definition. The word *technology* calls up very different images. If the term *tech toys* has you thinking of a computer or robot, you're a bit behind the times. It's really a much broader category than most parents realize. Today, technology has infused almost every category of toy, from dolls to construction toys to art supplies. Computer chips the size of a thumbnail can turn a traditional plush toy into an interactive experience. Such toys as remote-control vehicles and computer keyboards are available for the smallest consumers. The technology revolution has spread throughout toyland. There are even books with interactive elements. All these can be reasonably dubbed technology toys. All are somehow powered by a technological element, be it electricity, a battery, or a computer chip. The next sections review the major categories.

Interactive Toys

This is any toy—in any form—that interacts with the child during play. It can be anything from a keyboard-based spelling game to a doll that answers questions to a car that comes when you call. How do they work? Most are enabled by embedded computer chips. These technological "brains" give toys the capacity—albeit limited—to interact with humans. Some interactive toys require batteries. Interactive toys are one of the fastest-growing segments of the toy market and are often the most heavily promoted toys of the holiday season.

Pros Interactive toys can bring a new and exciting level of engagement to play. The interactivity of a toy can hold a child's interest and even challenge the child to experiment and reach for new levels of skill and ability.

Cons Interactive toys may seem to jump the border into reality, but they're still just machines and, as such, are limited. An interactive toy is only as creative as its creator, and often the play patterns of interactive toys are confined to

TOY TIP

Don't be too quick to jump on the bandwagon of any brand-new interactive toy system. It's not unusual for a toy company to roll out, for example, an interactive plush toy and a full line of accompanying CDs, cartridges, and such. The problem is that there's no guarantee that these systems will catch on and have a long-term presence in toy stores. So if you've invested a lot in the original toy, you may be disappointed when next year the company fails to come out with new games or a new way to play with the toy and leaves you (and your child) hanging. Best advice: try out any newcomer to the interactive scene carefully. Purchase some initial items, but save the whole-hog shopping trip for when the brand has a better track record.

the strict interpretation of the toy maker. This means that the way a child plays with the toy is pretty well set by its technology. In the instance of a creatively designed interactive toy, this limitation isn't a problem, but in the case of a less advanced product, you're looking at a short lived toy.

Computer Games

Once the exclusive territory of older kids and even young adults, computer games have evolved so that they now reach for all ages of game players. There are computer games designed for all children, teenagers to toddlers. How do they work? The games are played on a personal computer. There are two major segments—software games and online games. Software games require that you purchase the disc and install it at home to play. Although the game may have multiple skill levels and evolve with your child as he or she improves, the content of the game is limited to what's on the software when you buy it. Online games are somewhat different. In this segment, you access the game via the Internet. Often this requires registration and, in some cases, a subscription fee. Online games can be changed and updated by the site owners.

Pros   Sophisticated computer games can be great learning tools. There are computer games that teach academic skills, encourage problem solving, and engage children in a host of intellectually challenging activities. Little ones can learn early eye-hand coordination through the use of a mouse, and older kids will benefit from keyboard skills. Unlike television, computer games engage the user and demand focus, attention, and participation.

Cons   Not all computer games are well designed. For every engaging, exciting piece of software there is a lazily designed counterpart that simply flashes on the screen and does little to stimulate the attention of the game player. Such games are dull and often are quickly discarded, much to the dismay of the adult who shelled out double-digit sums for the item. Another concern: content. Not all computer games have age-appropriate content, and parents are often remiss by not carefully screening computer games—both software and online—for objectionable images or story lines.

TOY TIP

Make sure your family PC is up-to-date, with the latest (or nearly the latest) in video and audio cards as well as a current version of its operating system. Also, keep an eye on how much memory you need to run the new games. Often a brand-new game can't show its stuff on an older computer. In some cases, a new game won't run at all. Read the game package carefully for any technical requirements.

Game Systems

From the ranks of the great game companies, such as Nintendo, Sony, and Sega, comes the category of technology toy called *systems*. They're often referred to as "video games," although in many cases there's no actual video involved. How do you use them? Every system has two parts. You first need the system itself; it attaches to your television set. Second, you need the game cartridges. Major systems have many cartridges to choose from and often release much-hyped new games around each holiday season. Like their computer cousins, game systems have undergone significant evolution in recent years. Today, the graphics are intense, and the types of games are increasingly sophisticated. Many of the games require skill, strategy, and even practice. Some of the systems' most intense devotees are adult men. This is not simply child's play.

Pros Despite concerns about the amount of time kids spend in front of game systems, a recent study suggests

TOY TIP

Set specific and well-publicized rules about game system use. Decide on daily time limits. Decide how that time will be measured, such as by hourglass or egg timer. Decide how you will pick who plays first. Game systems can generate huge levels of family conflict if not monitored carefully. Tensions can run high between siblings and between parents and children. Set down your house rules and be firm. It will short-circuit some of the inevitable debate.

that these games aren't necessarily bad. Many of them can help enhance eye-hand coordination, and there's even some research that suggests a player can successfully confront phobias, such as fear of insects or heights, and other fears through video game playing. Used in moderation, these games have their place in healthy child development.

Cons   Many parents complain that the games are so engaging, they border on the addictive. It's not unusual for a child or even an adult to develop a near obsession with a video game system. Another problem is that time spent sitting on the sofa, eyes glued to the TV screen, is time lost to exercise and other physically healthy activity. Game systems must be monitored for overuse.

Remote-Control Toys

For parents of a certain generation, these will be the most familiar of the technology toys. Many of the elements remain the same. They tend to be vehicles (although animal

TOY TIP

After a while, a child may get tired of racing a remote-control toy back and forth across the driveway or hall. So come up with new ways to make the toy interesting. Set up obstacle courses. Make it a contest to see who can get the car through the maze in the shortest amount of time. Experiment with terrain and other variables.

and human forms are not unheard of). They are often powered by batteries. Their tricks involve movement rather than speech, and they're great for delighting a younger sibling or terrifying the family cat. The latest news in remote-control toys centers around its age groups. This was once a segment primarily for older children who could reliably work the gears. But toy makers have adapted remote-control technology to the point that tiny toddler hands can work the machinery. There are now remote-control toys for many different ages and stages.

Pros Thanks to improvements in technology, many younger children can experience the fun of remote control, and therein lies a great teaching tool. Remote-control toys certainly help develop understanding of cause and effect. As kids get older, their remote-control toys become more sophisticated and more complex in their movements, allowing kids to explore speed and physics through play.

Cons Most remote-control toys require some decent physical space for enjoyable play, which often means taking them outside. That means parental supervision.

Also, remote-control toys tend to need batteries. Be sure you have the correct batteries on hand when the toy is presented.

When to Use Tech Toys

Once you understand what you're looking at, the next step is to know when and why a particular technology toy is appropriate for your child. A lot will depend on that child's personality. Some children—like their adult counterparts—gravitate quickly to the mechanical. Others find that the tech elements leave them cold. So experiment with your child to find his or her comfort zone with technology toys. You can also apply some general age-and-stage guidelines, which we'll look at next. These will help you understand the way a technology element may affect your child's play.

Infants

Yes, there are technology-enhanced toys designed for babies. Scary? Well, no, not if you understand that the real market for infant tech toys is moms. In recent years, the toy market has come up with a new generation of infant toys that incorporate many new technology ideas—most of them primarily for mom's benefit.

Take, for example, the latest in infant crib entertainment systems. These will look familiar to the eye: they are designed to hang on the side of baby's crib, and with a variety of textures, visuals, sounds, and shapes, they are a great way for baby to entertain himself or herself for the few minutes it takes for mom to answer the phone or brush her teeth. Now, put technology into the picture. The new generation of these popular toys may have motion detection systems that allow baby to activate the toy with the wave of a tiny hand, or light and sound shows that perform on touch. Many of these elements are powered by internal chips that give the toy a longer and more engaging play pattern.

So, is this tech-enhanced toy better for baby? No. The old one did the same job. But for busy moms who may need the extra three minutes to care for a sibling, handle a household chore, or just sit down for a moment, the "teched-out" toy is a great innovation. Baby is entertained, and mom has a moment to recoup.

Another technology-enhanced toy for infants comes in the form of a licensed character doll that sings or dances. These toys are often powered by batteries, embedded computer chip, or both. Babies may delight in the sound and movement, and that's great. But keep in mind that the baby might have the same reaction if you were to position a tech-free doll and provide the singing and dancing accompaniment yourself. The technology element is mostly going to impress the parents. Now, if the technology element entertains the parent and encourages the adult to get down on the floor and play with baby, mission accomplished. In that case, the technology has fulfilled its goal: it has enhanced the playtime of an adult and child.

When buying a technology-enhanced toy for an infant, keep in mind whom it will really help. Don't be fooled by toy makers who suggest that a tech toy will speed your infant's intellectual development. That's not the case. But if a tech-enhanced toy makes the caregiver's life easier or encourages parents to interact with their infants more, then it's a perfectly good buy. Just don't expect tech toys to turn out baby geniuses. That's a sales pitch, not a scientific truth.

Toddlers

Toddlers and tech—it's a bit of a gray area. Toy makers have certainly put effort into creating and designing technology toys that toddler hands can operate. There are interactive toys, computer software, and other items designed with this age group in mind. But as parents you still have to navigate this landscape carefully. Just because a toddler *can* use a tech toy doesn't mean he or she *should*.

Take, for example, interactive plush toys or dolls. Your toddler may thrill to the response he or she gets from this enhanced toy. But the interactive animal has a downside: he comes programmed with a specific play pattern. This is not to say that a toddler can't deviate from the pattern and play a different way, but many won't. So the toy may have limited play value. The toddler may lose interest in the tech-guided toy. Or the toddler may fail to explore new play patterns because the toy doesn't suggest them. It's something to be aware of as a parent. Some toys have a lot of play potential, and technology can get in the way.

Other toys, though, are clearly enhanced by technology. Those that encourage a child to learn letter or number recognition are all the more engaging if they can speak to a child, sing or flash at a correct answer, and otherwise bring entertainment value to the learning experience. The key is to look at the toy and ask yourself, what does technology do for this toy? And is that going to improve or limit the experience for my child?

One great benefit of technology toys for toddlers is the ability they have to help teach cause and effect. Nothing is more obvious than the cause-and-effect nature of a tech toy. You command the toy with a button or your voice or remote control, and it responds. A well-designed toy may respond in different ways to different commands, which also has learning value. Be sure when you're choosing a technology-enhanced toy for a toddler that you give it the once-over for age appropriateness. Are the controls easy enough for somewhat clumsy toddler hands to manage? If the keyboard or controls are small or require too much dexterity, that's a downside. You should be able to operate the toy by giving it a good hard swipe. Anything more complicated may be suitable only for an older child. Also, is the response immediate? Toddlers are just learning the concept of two-step actions, so be sure the tech toy is not out of the reach of that level of understanding.

Finally, what about computers? Certainly, the computer industry has stepped up to serve the toddler market. There are scads of games designed for toddlers. There's even hardware for the toddler set—you can find a toddler-friendly mouse, a toddler-friendly keyboard, even ergonomic furniture for the toddler computer. And many parents report that their toddlers seem to love sitting on their laps, playing computer games.

No doubt, but it's likely that the key part of that enjoyment comes from the engagement between toddler and parent. The computer is just the prop. So it's fine if you want to sit your toddler up on your lap and play age-appropriate computer games together. Look for games that are simple for a toddler to follow, games that feature child-appropriate characters and situations and, even better, encourage early learning skills. But don't think that the computer is the only reason this great play moment is taking place. It's a perfectly fine way to play, if you and your child are enjoying it. But you're doing most of the great play work. The computer is just going along for the ride. No one has yet come up with software that will replace toddler time with mom and dad.

Preschool

The world of technology opens in a new way for preschool-age children. At ages three and four, kids understand how to make things "go," including computers, video games, and other technology-infused toys.

The good news is, this is the age when a good supply of technology toys full of education and fun is available. Traditional board games may incorporate tech elements to play music or interact with the players. Computer games teach early reading and math skills, and enhance the lessons with favorite characters and songs. Music toys can encourage composition and even employ technology to record and play back musical creations. Technology can add a new level of enjoyment to many traditional preschool toys. The key is to pick toys in which the technology enhances, not overwhelms, the toy. If the tech element—say, the song or interactivity—is the sole reason to play the game, it may not be a great toy. Once the novelty of the tech trick wears off, that toy is destined for the back of the closet. Look for preschool toys in which the technology element is just that—an element—of an otherwise great toy.

Does a preschooler need his or her own computer? Probably not. Although a child this age may show a lot of enthusiasm for computers and games, it's not the right time to set up his own machine. First of all, a parent will still need to supervise preschooler computer time. A child this age is not old enough to manage most games alone, so if you've set him up in his own room, you'll have to run in there every five minutes or so to troubleshoot. The computer in the family room should be just fine for preschooler use. And if that's not an option, public libraries also offer computers for children's use. Don't worry that your child isn't getting enough computer time. Despite the news that tech skills are in hot demand, few economists are suggesting that preschoolers need to learn keyboard skills to gain an edge in the job market.

A word about computer games and education: there are many great computer games that encourage learning. But resist the temptation to turn all play into a pseudo classroom experience. Don't forget that pure play—even without an obvious teaching element—is learning as well. Computers tend to bring out the inner teacher in many parents. Be sure you are not being too prescriptive with your computer game choices. You don't want your child developing the notion that the computer is nothing but work.

School Age

This is often an unnerving period in the parent-child tech relationship. This is the age when the children will begin to outstrip the parents in terms of knowledge and ability. As your children enter school, the news they'll get about technology will soon have them dancing circles around you. Be prepared. And hang on. This is a time when your involvement in their technology choices will be more critical than ever.

First off, keep a sharp eye on game content. Be vigilant in your supervision of the content of technology games—everything from the story line of a handheld game to the way the characters are dressed in a video game. Many of these games have violent story lines or visuals unsuitable for children. And don't just take a cursory look at the game and consider your job done. Play it through to the end. Know the story line and content of the games your child wants to play.

Second, manage your child's technology time. Although some computer and tech-related play is fine, you don't want it to substitute for other activities that are crucial to a school-age child, such as social play with a peer or physical exercise. Set time limits and be firm. Twenty minutes of computer game play is a good rule of thumb, but you will have to come up with rules that work for your family and your child.

Finally, perhaps your most important duty during this stage in your child's technology play is to instill the family technology values. Your child is approaching the age when he or she will meet technology without you in the room. Children encounter games at the homes of their friends, in schools or libraries, and at home when you're not there. You need to be clear and consistent with your child about what you expect in terms of technology play. You may decide you don't want your child playing certain game systems. Or you may want your child to seek permission before trying a new game. You may want to be with your child when he or she plays any games online or plays Internet games that involve more than one player. You need to put some effort into understanding your own thinking around technology and convey that to your child.

Technology Toy FAQs

More questions? No problem.

Will all the various screens—computer terminals, TV screens, tiny handheld screens—do damage to children's eyes?

It's true that too much screen time can cause eye strain. To combat this, makes sure your child breaks up screen time by looking away for a bit. Also, set time limits on games that use screens.

Do computer games really help hand-eye coordination?

Recent studies on the subject do suggest that kids who play these games do develop these skills.

Can computer games help my child overcome certain fears?

A recent report on computer games found that psychologists were able to use them to help individuals cope with certain phobias, such as fear of insects or heights. However, this is not the kind of project a parent should undertake without supervision. If you feel your child has a fear that needs intervention, consult your child's doctor or a psychology professional. Don't go looking for help in the game aisle.

Do technology toys stifle creativity?

Sort of, but it's not as simple as that. Certainly, technology toys have more specific and set play patterns than other kinds of toys. A toy with a tech feature may lend itself to a particular kind of play. That does limit imagination in some respects. However, there are more kinds of play than just imaginative play. A child should be exposed to both open-ended imaginative play and the more structured play pattern of a technology toy. Both have benefits. Neither is inherently better than the other.

Are there commercial messages hidden in computer and video games?

Yes, and they're not so well hidden, either. More and more game makers are opening up their platforms to advertising and marketing content. It is not unusual to find a computer game that actually encourages players to go see a certain movie or buy a particular toy or fast-food item. What's more, many advertising companies have learned to design games that incorporate their clients' products. One very popular online game site for kids features different kinds of candy—brand names explicitly displayed—as elements of a game. That's a never-ending commercial. Be sure you look at and play the games your child is enjoying and be prepared to respond to the ad messages embedded in the content.

Should my child have her own computer?

Depends on the age of the child. Certainly a young child—under ten—does not need her own personal computer. It should be fine to share the family PC or even use the computer at school or the library. By junior high school, kids may have more use for a computer for schoolwork and for fun and games. So it's fine to consider one at that age, but don't feel compelled to send the family into debt for it. It's not a must-have; it's a nice extra. Toddlers and preschoolers do not need their own computers, despite what you may see in the computer stores. What little use they can get out of a machine designed for grown-up use they can get while sitting in your den or home office. You do not give your preschooler an edge by setting her up with her own home office.

My child has a computer. Where should it be set up?

Many parents put computers in a child's room without a second thought. In fact, the older your child gets, the more you will want his computer to be out someplace in the common family space. You want your child to know that whatever he is doing on the computer, you can see it. You can't supervise if the child and his computer are behind a closed door.

Do predators really lure children via computers?

Yes. By masquerading as other kids or teens, predators are frequently able to engage unsuspecting children in online conversations and even are able to arrange face-to-face meetings. Be sure to monitor your child's online communication and teach your child that "stranger danger" issues apply online.

Will interactive toys help my baby develop skills at a faster rate?

It's unlikely. Some toys may magnify skills, but the acquisition of skills is often a physical process. No toy will cause your child's brain to develop at a faster rate of speed.

Will technology toys give my child an edge in school?

That depends on the toy. Some educational games may help your child practice and retain certain school-related skills. For example, if your child is learning multiplication at school, a game or toy that encourages similar math skills will help solidify and reinforce the classroom teaching.

Conclusion

Technology toys offer a host of benefits when properly managed. The key is to avoid becoming so enthralled by the bells and whistles that you forget to evaluate them as you would any other toy: on the basis of fun and usability for your own child. Children today will grow up in a world where technology is a given. Making smart choices about technology toys starts them off on the right track.

WORKSHEET

Technology Troubleshooting

So you have a new computer game, you've popped it into the PC, and it won't run. What could be wrong? Before you take it back to the store, run through this checklist and see if you can solve the problem yourself.

- Check the power source. There may be a cable or wire detached.
- Reboot the PC. Turning it off and on again may rectify your glitch.
- Read both the hard-copy and online instructions. They should be the same, but sometimes they're not. Your answer may be in the format you haven't reviewed.
- Do you have the latest video driver? If not, that may be the reason your PC is not displaying the new game. Check to see if you need to download the updated version.
- Check the game website. Often game sites will offer live chat, email help services, and more specific troubleshooting suggestions.

Tales from the Toy Tips Lab

When we tell parents they have to screen the entire game or video for objectionable content, we are not kidding around. Once we were testing a game, and deep into play—on one of the advanced levels of the game—we were completely surprised to find an image of a scantily clad woman dancing across the game screen. No mention of *that* on the box. Unless you've played the game, you have no idea what your child may see or hear.

Chapter 6

Health and Safety

Any parent will tell you: children have a re-
markable talent for getting into trouble. No
matter how you baby-proof, kid-test, and try
to prepare, children are curious creatures. And sometimes
a little one's curiosity can be hazardous to his or her
health, even when engaged in the most child-friendly of
activities, such as playing with toys.

No toy is 100 percent, guaranteed, foolproof safe.
There's just no such thing. No design, label, material, or
manufacturer's promise can make that happen. There are
always ways a child can find to get hurt with a toy. So no
matter what you may learn about the best ways to buy
safe and healthy toys, remember: you must always supervise your children when they play with toys. That's the nature of accidents and certainly the nature of life with a
child. No manufacture's label will absolve you of the re-
sponsibility of proper supervision.

Still, the level and type of supervision needed will
evolve and change with your child and the toys involved.
Your efforts will depend on the age and stage of the child
and the nature of the toy itself. A baby may need to be in
view and at arm's length when playing with a toy. A school-
age child may simply need clear and specific instructions
on allowable play. The key is knowing where the hazards
may hide and how to protect against them. There's no
value in hovering constantly—that can quickly take the
fun out of playtime. Instead, when it comes to health and
safety issues, be prepared, think ahead, and do what you
can to head off potential problems before they arise.

What follows is a discussion of common toy-related hazards and the ages at which they are most likely to occur. It is by no means exhaustive—children will always think up a new way to get into a fix. You are the best judge of what your child may or may not do with a toy. But this discussion is a good place to start and will help you formulate your own plan for staying ahead of hazards.

It bears repeating: nothing substitutes for parental supervision. You need to know your child's abilities and developmental stage, and you need to set and enforce appropriate rules and supervision. That's your job. What follows is information that can help you do it well.

Newborns

Chances are, your infant has been showered with toys by well-wishing friends and relatives. But not all toys are safe for newborns. In fact, some toys need to sit safely out of reach for many months before your little one can play with them alone. There are several important health and safety issues to consider when matching toys with infants.

Suffocation

That oversized teddy bear is very cute, but it's not safe for an infant. Newborn babies who do not have the ability yet to roll over, sit up, or use their arms and legs to move reliably are at risk of suffocation. Don't put stuffed animals in a crib with baby. If you want your child to see and interact with a stuffed animal, make the toys part of parental play moments. Get down on the floor with your child and the stuffed toys, and you can introduce your baby to the wonders of a plush toy. But do not leave your baby alone

TOY TIP

The best way to guard against injury to an infant is to be in the room with the baby during playtime. If you must answer the doorbell or move to another part of the home, bring baby with you. If you have placed the baby in a crib, be very careful about the toys within baby's reach. A mobile or cribside entertainment system that is securely fastened so that baby can't move it is a good bet. But stuffed animals and other toys that baby can reach and move can be hazardous and shouldn't be left alone with the baby. Keep these items for playtime you share together.

with a stuffed toy. Instead, keep the toys on a shelf or in a toy box and bring them out for supervised play.

Sharp Edges

You pad the corners of your coffee table and other furniture. Have you checked toys for sharp edges? Consider two possibilities: sharp edges can be a hazard on a large toy, one that a baby might bump up against; they may also be a hazard on a smaller toy, one that baby might pick up and bonk against his head or eye. Even toys obviously designed for children may still have sharp edges. Board books, for example, should have rounded corners. A clean right angle cut can be hazardous in the unreliable grip of a baby.

Choking

Even if you think your baby is not yet at the put-everything-in-her-mouth-stage, you should be on the lookout for choking hazards. The baby's not going to send you a telegram alerting you when she has reached the new developmental stage. It's your job to be ready. When you are giving a new doll or toy to baby, take all small pieces off. Choking hazards on a doll or stuffed animal include socks or shoes, buttons, glued-on eyes, bells, and jewelry. Also, be aware of the toys that belong to older siblings. They too must be inspected for choking hazards. When unwrapping gifts, be sure to discard all packaging before sitting down to play.

Older Babies

At about six months, baby's skills take a developmental leap, and a new world opens up. Now sitting, reaching, grabbing, and even starting to pull up and crawl, baby will be able to do a host of new things and enjoy new toys. With this newfound mobility comes a new set of health and safety issues.

Choking

This is commonly the age when babies begin to explore using all their senses, and mouthing is a very popular exploration tactic. Many babies at this age will greet a new or interesting object by seeing first if it fits in the mouth. Also, in the second half of the first year, baby may begin to sprout teeth, providing yet another impetus to mouth and chew toys. Remove all small parts from toys and dolls. Be aware that the game pieces and toys of older siblings

TOY TIP

Be careful at this age to supervise baby in his or her interactions with siblings or other older children. A baby that is just learning to crawl, pull up, and grab is old enough to annoy an older child. That may result in the older sibling's giving the baby a swat or push. Be aware that the emerging mobility of your baby means he or she can get into an older child's space for the first time. The older child may be surprised and dismayed to discover that the infant who used to just lie there can now move, pull, and grab. Be vigilant when the two meet during playtime.

dangerous if a parent forgets the number one rule of baby play and leaves baby unattended in one of these motion toys. Although the baby may seem secure and happy, the toys are not meant to substitute for your presence. Injuries can occur when babies are left alone in anything that moves. Baby gates and other safety items are a good idea, but they are not foolproof. A baby in motion must always be supervised.

Toddlers

It's hard to find a parent of a toddler not highly tuned to health and safety issues. Toddlers are walking disasters in the making. With their newfound mobility and inquisitive natures, they barrel into all kinds of trouble. Toys are no

are also a hazard. Buttons or other brightly col[...]
may look like candy. Instruct anyone who superv[...]
child, be it a babysitter or relative, that all toys [...]
thoroughly inspected for choking hazards before ba[...]
play. Generally, any item smaller than a table ten[...]
should not be in baby's hands.

Toxicity

Because more objects are likely to end up in baby's mo[...]
at this stage, another hazard comes into play: potenti[...]
poisonings or toxicity. Know what your child's toys ar[...]
made of and be sure you understand whether or not the
materials are toxic. Most toys made for babies and toddlers are made with nontoxic materials. If you're not sure,
read the box, quiz the manufacturer, and check with your
pediatrician—better safe than sorry. Be aware that heirloom toys may have been produced in an era when lead-
based paint was still in use. So a doll from your childhood
may be better placed on the shelf for decoration rather
than in the playpen for playtime.

When it comes to toxicity, get your information from
credible sources. It's not uncommon for unfounded reports
of toxicity and other dangers to crop up on the Internet or
via email chain letters. These are at best unreliable sources
and at worst hoaxes. Ask your child's doctor if you are at
all unsure.

Baby in Motion

There are some toys and baby gear that are made to entertain babies through movement, such as swings, bouncy
seats, walkers, or even spinning saucers. They can be

exception. As your little one is walking, exploring, and doing everything he or she can to be a big kid, be on the lookout for toy-related hazards.

Choking

You may think your child is past the put-everything-in-his-mouth stage, but that's not necessarily so. Choking is still a danger to any child. Remove the dangling pieces of any doll or toy. Resist the urge to give kids complicated puzzle pieces and detailed construction sets; they are not appropriate for children under three. Stick to the ones with large, chunky pieces. Give firm, consistent instruction regarding common items such as crayons and chalk—they're for playing, not for eating—and supervise drawing sessions.

Furniture or Toy Storage Injuries

Your child is fully mobile and has an independent mind. That means you must think about the safety of not only the toys themselves but also their storage. Shelves can be scaled like ladders. Toy boxes can be opened and closed by determined toddler hands. Closet door knobs can be turned. However you have stored toys, be sure you have taken precautions to make the storage safe. Choose toy boxes with spring-resistant lids that won't smash down on tiny fingers. Consider bolting shelves to the wall so they can't be toppled—or keep toys down low to discourage climbing. Be certain that closet doors can't lock your curious toddler inside.

TOY TIP

Scan your home and neighborhood for safe play spaces. They may be the child's room, a family room, a local playground, or an indoor play space. Toddlers are always on the move, and they need room to roam. You need an inventory of safe spaces so that you and your toddler won't become bored in the same old baby-proofed bedroom.

Germs

Parents may spend adequate time making toys safe, but they should put additional effort, especially in the toddler years, to making them healthy. Toys are a prime means of spreading germs. Toddlers should not share toys that come in contact with hands and mouths. Toys should be washed regularly, using a 50-50 bleach-and-water solution for plastic items and the washer and dryer for plush. For stuffed toys that can't handle the washing machine, even the dryer will help cut down on allergens, so send them through.

Preschool

At this age, your child is old enough to play games, create art, and act out any manner of story or drama. He or she can hear and understand your instructions. Supervision now means careful explanation of what toys are for, how they are and are not to be played with, and what rules surround their use. Be clear and consistent in your instructions to your preschooler and be aware of the common hazards that crop up at this age.

Activity Accidents

Often at this age, children will start to express an interest in craft kits and activity toys. Children benefit from creative play. But supervise these kinds of toys closely because they can present hazards. Read the box carefully to be sure that all the items your child will handle are made from nontoxic materials. Be sure to supervise so that any tools—such as scissors—and materials are used appropriately. Also, store any leftover materials away from your preschooler's reach. Be aware that some children may have skin rashes or other negative reactions when encountering craft materials for the first time.

Playground Injuries

Preschoolers are often fearless climbers, and they love to test their skills on the playground. Be sure that yours passes safety inspection. Are the climbing structures in good repair? Are they free from rust or peeling paint? Are surfaces under the climbing structures able to absorb impact should a child fall? Are sandboxes cleaned regularly? (They are prime hiding places for all sorts of nasty bugs and bacteria.) Check out the playground you take your child to and also visit any other play areas your child may frequent in a preschool or playgroup. Although you can't prevent every bump and bruise, be sure you can see your child on the playground at all times. If the child is out of view, go investigate.

TOY TIP

As much as you work to keep your child safe, you must also work to keep other children safe from your child. This means stating, repeating, and enforcing rules of play. When your child tests the boundaries of behavior by pushing another child or swiping a toy, you must be firm and clear with your instructions. This is an age when behavioral rules can begin to be enforced. Be sure you are as concerned about the safety of your child's playmates as you are for that of your own child.

Combat Injuries

The preschool world is a hands-on experience. Children this age begin to play the interactive games that will teach them about social relationships. So tag and other run-and-chase games are common and require some supervision. You don't want to take all the fun out of the game, but pay attention so that children don't turn otherwise harmless items like paintbrushes and construction blocks into dangerous projectiles as they chase each other around.

School Age

As they grow, children require less hands-on supervision as they play, but certainly health and safety issues still arise. At this age, you can expect your child to understand

and obey any health and safety rules you set, and you as the parent must be prepared to discuss your reasons for any rules. "Because I said so" isn't likely to inspire cooperation. Involve your child in the decision to play safely.

Riding Injuries

When it comes to bicycles, skateboards, scooters, skates, and anything else with wheels, be sure your child wears proper safety gear. A helmet that fits well and does not slip around on the child's head is a must. And any helmet that has been in an accident involving serious impact should be replaced. Knee and elbow pads protect against abrasions. Wrist guards are useful for in-line skaters most at danger of a forward fall. Remind your child that safety gear only goes so far and that safety rules must apply so that he or she can avoid injuries. Instruct your child to ride only in approved areas and to stay out of the street or any other trafficked area (such as a parking lot).

Technology Injuries

Just like adults, children can have technology-related health problems. Too much time in front of a computer or video game can result in eye strain. Set appropriate time limits on game play and encourage your child to look up and away from the screen at regular intervals. Also, repetitive stress injuries are not unheard of in school-age children. If your child is complaining about wrist, elbow, neck, or shoulder pain, consider the computer setup. Is the chair adjustable? Is the monitor at a good height for the child? Does the game your child plays require a

TOY TIP

Make sure the homes your child visits for play dates are safe. Sometimes parents are hesitant to ask questions because they fear being tagged as nosy or overprotective. But strike a positive, friendly tone and talk to the parents of your child's playmates. Ask these questions: Will you be supervising our children during the play date, or will others such as a babysitter or older sibling be asked to supervise? Will the children be at your home or at another location? Do you have a dog? A swimming pool? Are you confident that these potential safety hazards have been made secure?

constant pounding on the keyboard? All of these should be considered.

Sports Injuries

As children grow into school age they are more apt to be engaged in competitive sports. There are several important health and safety issues to consider when your child competes. Learn about the program and the coach in charge. Does the coach lead kids in a warm-up? Does the program use and encourage the use of safety equipment? Are kids taught proper skills to avoid injuries? Does someone on the team staff have appropriate training in first aid? Team sports are great fun. Be sure your child's chosen sport is run safely and wisely.

Special Health and Safety Situations

Some toys come with their own set of health and safety issues. This doesn't mean they must be banned. Instead, they must be appropriately supervised, managed, and stored so that they can be enjoyed safely.

Heirloom Toys

You may have a favorite doll or train set from your childhood. Or there may even be toys in your family that have been passed down through generations. Heirloom toys make wonderful connections between parents and children, even grandparents and grandchildren. They are often the foundation of marvelous intergenerational playtime and memories. But because these toys were crafted in an era before current safety standards were in place, it pays to give them a careful inspection.

- *What kind of paint has been used?* In previous generations, it was not uncommon to use lead-based paint even in the crafting of toys and playthings. Its harmful effects were not well known. So a painted toy made years ago, such as a train or dollhouse, must be inspected for chips and other signs of paint wear. These toys should be displayed and not used as playthings.
- *Has age made the toy dangerous?* A toy that was perfectly safe twenty years ago may now be more fragile, so parts that were once securely fastened may now be in danger of coming loose. Inspect the toy for elements that could come loose and become a choking hazard.

TOY TIP

Consider making heirloom toys the focus of family playtime—moments when you will be with your child to supervise the toy's use. Doing so will help keep your child safe from any potential hazards and will also protect the toy. Heirloom toys often have great sentimental value. In the hands of an unsupervised small child, a treasured toy can be ruined. So for everyone's peace of mind, make heirloom toys special for family time.

- *Is it age appropriate?* Time can blur the memory a bit. Perhaps you remember playing with a particular toy as a child—but how old were you really? Sometimes, motivated by a desire to share a treasured toy with our children, we offer up train sets and china dolls before they are age appropriate. A toy will be best enjoyed when a child is developmentally ready to play with it. Don't rush the heirloom toys out of the attic. Wait until your child has reached the stage to truly appreciate your gift.

Battery-Operated Toys

When it comes to keeping battery-powered toys safe, the key is to make sure the batteries stay in the toy, where they belong. It is remarkably easy to remove the batteries of some toys, creating a safety hazard you must watch for. Batteries contain acid, and children should not handle them. Although it is rare that a battery opens and leaks, it

TOY TIP

Keep extra batteries on hand. Some toys drain power remarkably quickly. In some tests, it took only a few hours before the toy lost juice. Especially when it's a new toy and likely to get a lot of initial play, have a backup power pack handy. Be sure to follow the battery-charging guidelines provided by the manufacturer. Charge a battery overnight for a first-time use. This enables maximum battery capacity. Also, never leave a battery in the charger; continuous charging shortens battery life.

is quite dangerous when it does happen, and you should not take that chance.

When buying a battery-operated toy, inspect the battery compartment. The best kinds are those that must be opened by a no. 0 or no. 1 Philips screwdriver. These may take a little extra time on your part, but it's worth it. If the battery compartment can be opened by hand, it should be sufficiently difficult that a toddler can't manage it. Rest assured, if the battery compartment can be opened by a child, a child will open it and explore the contents. At best, that can result in lost batteries. At worst, batteries can present a true danger to children if improperly handled.

TVs and Videos

You may not consider your television a toy, but it's likely your child does. Parents today often allow their child considerable access to the family television set, VCR, and

TOY TIP

When it comes to play dates or other times a child may visit your home, save the videos and DVDs for the end of the playtime, when the children may be winding down and in need of some quiet time. If you bring the videos out too early, the children may simply stop playing with one another and watch the screen. Time the videos to dovetail with the play date's natural rhythm.

video storage area. Smart toddlers can learn to choose their favorite tapes, pop them in, even work the buttons on the VCR with ease. You should therefore inspect and supervise your television and video equipment as you do any other plaything your child comes in contact with.

- *The TV stand.* Emergency rooms frequently see children who have been injured by a falling television. Be sure your television is on a stable piece of furniture—one that can't topple or be made unsteady by a two-year-old. Be sure cords and other enticing elements are out of sight and out of reach. Consider a cabinet or other container that keeps the television away from your child.
- *Video storage.* If you choose a high shelf, you run the risk that one day your child will opt to use it as a ladder. Store videos out of sight to reduce the risk, or consider storing them at floor level for safe access.
- *The clicker is not at toy!* You may have said this a thousand times, but children will still want to handle the remote control. Be certain that yours is either child-

proof—meaning that the batteries can't come out and it has no small parts that can come loose—or keep it someplace your child can't get to.

Allergies

If your child is sniffling, consider the toy box as a potential culprit. Toys are a prime hiding place for allergens such as mold and dust mites. Be sure that plastic toys are

 # TOY TIP

Commercial modeling dough can sometimes be a source of skin rashes in allergic children. Consider making your own so that you can control the ingredients (see recipe). Other craft items may also irritate a sensitive child's skin. If you see skin rashes, consider items such as paints or clays as potential culprits. Some children are particularly sensitive to dyes, for example, or preservative ingredients used in mass manufacturing. Catalogues that sell environmentally friendly products are a good place to look for alternatives.

Modeling Dough Recipe
1 c. flour
½ c. salt
3 tbls. vegetable oil
½ c. hot water

Mix well.

washed regularly. Use a 50-50 solution of water and bleach to kill germs. For plush items, a full cycle through the washer and dryer is best, but be sure to check the label first. If the toy won't stand up to the washing machine, a spin through the dryer alone will at least help cut down on the allergens.

Recalls

At every change of season, it is a good idea to check for recalls of potentially hazardous toys that you may have in your home. Recalls are continuously posted, and you can log on to recalls.gov or toytips.com for current information.

Conclusion

Although many toy makers have taken steps to make their wares safe, ultimately ensuring the health and safety of your child falls to you. This is as it should be—you are best equipped to get the job done right. So consider toy makers your associates in creating safe and healthy play, but consider yourself the boss. Accidents may happen; you can't prevent every bump and bruise. But a watchful eye and up-to-date knowledge can help you be prepared and get ahead of many possible hazards.

WORKSHEET

Toy Cleaning Checklist

At every change of season, revisit your child's toy box
with a cleaning crew. Here's what to do:

- Put all rattles and other mouthing toys in the dishwasher.
  (This should be done regularly.) Most plastic and vinyl
  toys are dishwasher safe—but check the packaging.
- Gather all plastic and vinyl toys. Mix 1 cup of baking
  soda and 2 tablespoons of dishwashing liquid to make
  a cleaning paste. Clean all toys, scrubbing off any marks.
  Wipe clean with a sponge. Rubbing alcohol and nail pol-
  ish remover may get stains out of plastic toys, but be
  sure to keep these and other cleaning solutions out of
  the reach of children.
- Send plush toys through the washer and dryer. If the toy
  is not machine washable, use the dryer alone.
- To combat dust mites in plush toys, put the stuffed toy
  in a plastic bag and place in the freezer overnight. De-
  frost the toy before returning it to your child.
- Wash outdoor toys with soap and water.
- Use antibacterial wipes on toys.

Tales from the Toy Tips Lab

I got a call one day from an irate parent. She had purchased a new baby seat. While she was out of the room, her baby had pinched a finger in the seat workings. Luckily the baby was not seriously hurt. But the mother was furious that the product was on the market and wanted advice on how to get it recalled. I reminded her that my recommendation included the warning never to leave a baby unsupervised and that the same recommendation was printed on the box. I sympathize with busy parents. I'm a busy parent myself. But no object has yet been invented that can substitute for a parent's careful supervision of a child.

Chapter 7

Smart Shopping

Time to go to the toy store.

If the very thought of entering a toy retailing establishment brings on a migraine, you're not alone. The toy store, though seemingly a happy and fun-filled place, is for many a shopper's nightmare. Aisles and aisles of gleaming packaging and enticing promotions. Shelves piled high with mysterious merchandise. And then there's the ambiance: fellow shoppers, stressed out and elbowing their way through their gift lists. Moms with crying children in tow. And checkout lines that snake back to the loading dock.

Pass the Excedrin.

Or, get smart. Toy shopping is a lot easier if you know how to beat the retailers at their game. Wandering into the store unprepared is a setup not just for a poor shopping experience but also, in all likelihood, poorly chosen toys. The most successful toy buyer arrives at the store prepared, shops the aisles like a pro, and leaves happy. It can be done. It just takes a little background in Toy Retailing 101.

Step One: Before You Go

Your shopping trip begins long before you leave the house. The first mistake most toy shoppers make is entering the retail establishment without having done the proper research. You don't need a dissertation to get started—just a little basic prep.

- *Review the toy box.* Take a moment to do an inventory of what your child already has. Look through the box and shelves and think back over recent months: Which toys have gotten a lot of play? Which ones have sat in here gathering dust? Also, think through, Which of these toys has my child already mastered? That will give you some ideas for magnifying and supplementing recently acquired play skills. Finally, look around and be honest: Which toys did you think would be big hits but in fact turned out to be duds? Make a promise to avoid that kind of toy again this trip, no matter how alluring the packaging or inexpensive the deal.

- *Make your list.* After each child's name, put his or her age, skills, and interests. If you have a toy in mind, great. Jot it down so you won't blank out at the store. If not, at least come to some decision about the category in which you will shop for a gift. Simply wandering the aisles hoping the great toy will jump out at you is a terrible strategy. It only guarantees that your choice will be driven by eye-catching packaging or sheer desperation on your part. Have at least a general idea before you hit the store.

- *Quiz the relatives.* If you're buying for a child you don't know well, pick up the phone and ask for some general information, such as recently acquired skills or hobbies. It takes only a minute to find out that your niece has just learned to cartwheel or your best friend's son loves monster trucks. You don't need a lot of information—just a few tips will do.

- *Cruise the "hot toys" lists.* Don't be fooled—those magazine articles and TV spots are probably not going to give you the scoop on the "best" toys. List makers certainly don't know what's best for your child. Most toy

TOY TIP

If at all possible, don't take your children on a toy-shopping trip. Unless you are prepared to buy for them on the spot, it's only a setup for disaster. There's almost no way a child can resist multiple aisles of brand-new toys. It's almost unfair to ask. These items are designed and packaged to be appealing to children. Children are only human. See if you can find time to shop when they're otherwise occupied. If you must have children in tow, explain in advance of arrival at the store that you will be shopping for other children and encourage your child to assist you. You can use this time to discuss with your child the importance of giving as well as receiving.

lists compiled by the media are quite unscientific in their approach. But what these lists do accomplish is round up the latest information on new toys. Check out the lists to see what might look promising for a child on your own list.

- **_Double dip._** You may be on your way to the store for a birthday gift, but are there other occasions looming on the horizon? One way to reduce toy shopping stress is to shop less often. If you can consolidate your efforts by shopping for more than one item per trip, you can cut back on your days spent navigating the wonderful world of toy retailing. Take out your calendar and think ahead so you can accomplish more than one toy buy in a trip.

- ***Set a budget.*** You may not stick to it, but at least you'll try. Without a budget as a guiding principle, you may wind up with sticker shock at the cash register. At that point, it may be too late to turn back and start again.

- ***Choose your time of day carefully.*** The smart time to shop varies by store, neighborhood, and time of year. Some stores are jammed on the weekends but peaceful and serene on any given weeknight. Some stores are wall-to-wall shoppers on a weekday lunch hour but empty on Sundays. Know your local retail trends. Is your store of choice in a suburban shopping mall? A downtown retail center? A popular tourist spot? All are crowded—and calm—at different times. If possible, pick a down time to hit the store. Your blood pressure will thank you for it.

Step Two: Consult the Map

Store design is a highly developed science. Researchers have spent years of study and millions of dollars to determine how to construct a store most conducive to buying. Ever wonder why milk is always in the farthest corner of the supermarket? That's to make sure that you walk past all the other aisles of goodies on your way to make that one purchase. That science is certainly at work in toy stores, too. Although different stores have different design strategies, you can bet that they're set up to present maximum buying opportunities. Here's what you need to know to make it work for you:

- ***Enter—then stop.*** Before you start roaming the aisles, pause a moment at the threshold and consider your options. You may be able to spot your aisle of choice. Or

TOY TIP

Beware the checkout line. The path to the cash register is paved with trinkets and doodads and knickknacks designed to tempt you even though you've finished your shopping and are prepping to pay. Don't buy what you don't need just because it's there and the cashier is taking ages with the customer in front of you.

you may see a store map to guide you. Don't stumble in and wander along. It's not very efficient.

- *Check the circular.* Major toy stores and discount chains may have a weekly circular at the front of the store. It's a good place to check for last-minute bargains and specials of the day.
- *Look high and low.* Once you're in the aisles, don't limit yourself to shelves at eye level. Stores make good use of their air space.
- *Check out the end caps.* That's the display of items at the end of each aisle. Often this is the space reserved for "loss leaders"—merchandise priced low to entice buyers. Don't miss the potential bargain.
- *Don't forget the nontoys.* There are several items crucial to happy gift giving that you may overlook. Be sure to consider purchasing a no. 0 or no. 1 screwdriver for toy assembly, batteries, an air pump, and antibacterial wipes to remove factory debris. Be sure to keep all these items away from children.

Step Three: Know Your Store Types

Toy store is actually a generic term for a varied category. There are many places to buy great toys. Some are traditional and some quite modern in their construct. No matter where you choose to shop, it pays to know the venue's pros and cons so that you can make an informed decision.

Here are the major players:

- *Discount chains.* In the past ten years, the rise of the national discount chain stores has had a major effect on the toy retailing industry. These are now the biggest sellers of toys in the country. They maintain toy departments year-round and expand them significantly during the fourth-quarter holiday season. What's good about them? The national chains have close ties to major toy manufacturers and are likely to have a good supply of the most popular toys. Also, they are fiercely competitive and will often have prices designed to keep you from wandering across the mall parking lot to the competition. The downside? They don't carry a deep selection; generally only the most popular items get shelf space. So if you're looking for something unusual or unique, you probably won't find it in the discount aisles. Also, the sales help in a discount store are unlikely to have a lot of specific toy knowledge. Don't bother asking the sales clerk for a recommendation.
- *Category killers.* These freestanding big-box stores that specialize in toys used to rule the roost. Today they have a lot of competition, but they are still a good bet for the toy shopper. Pros: selection—lots of it. These are the stores that pride themselves on stocking anything and

everything. So if your list is long and varied, this may be a good spot to shop. This is also a good spot to find both the classics as well as the latest from the toy makers. Cons: this is the kind of store that nightmares are made of. It can be confusing to navigate and jammed to the rafters during peak holiday shopping times.

- *High-end specialty stores.* For the discerning toy shopper, the stand-alone specialty shop is a welcome retreat from the hustle and bustle of the major chain stores. Specialty shops tend to offer a limited selection of higher-end toys. Here you'll find dolls of collectible quality, unique and creative items a larger store might overlook, hard-to-find specialty toys that stand apart from their mass-market counterparts. Why shop here? The biggest asset is service. A high-end specialty shop is more likely to have courteous and knowledgeable service on hand. If you're in need of advice and guidance in the store itself, this may be your best choice. The downside? The price tag. No discounts here.

- *Department stores.* In the old days, these were Toy Central. Department stores were hosts to extensive toy departments, and during the holiday season the toy-related merchandise was a dominant theme in any department store's marketing plan. But times have changed. Department stores have for the most part exited the year-round toy business. However, many will still put up seasonal toy departments during the holiday season. These are good spots to look for classic toys and also for items that are custom made for the particular department store chain. Pros: if classic toys are on your list, the department store is a good pick. Cons: these stores have neither the selection nor style of yesteryear.

- ***Online stores.*** You don't save money on toys on the Internet. That's a big misconception. The Internet is a lot of things: fast, easy, and convenient, with selection galore. But it's not the best place to shop for toy bargains. Most of the online toy stores are extensions of traditional stores, and they're unlikely to undercut the prices marked on store shelves. Also, when you buy on the Internet, in all likelihood you'll pay a shipping charge. So if you spy a toy that looks cheap, mentally add shipping charges and see if it's still a bargain. Why shop online? One big reason: you can shop in complete silence. Just boot up the computer when the kids are in bed and hey, presto, a trip to the toy store sans headache. That alone has helped build online toy sales to a respectable level. Cons: lack of service; hidden charges; no guarantee that the item will arrive on time. And there's always the possibility that your online store will disappear into cyberspace.

- ***Catalogues.*** Like online stores, catalogues can't be beat for convenience and ease of use. In fact, many shoppers combine the store types by browsing through a paper catalogue and then logging on to make a purchase. Some multichannel merchants even make this easy by allowing you to shop by product code online; it's often very quick. Another plus to a catalogue: for older kids, it's a great way to open a discussion about what they'd really like. With a child preschool age or older, you can sit down and read the catalogue together, even using bookmark tape to mark key pages. Unlike the supercharged atmosphere of the toy store (where kids are hard pressed to act rationally), your living room sofa affords a quiet place for a conversation about what might be fun and what toys are most appealing to your child.

TOY TIP

Know your complaint and return options. A local store may be more open to your concerns than a chain. A land-based store may be easier to buttonhole than a virtual merchant. Understand the various ways your store of choice will interact with you if something should turn out not to be to your liking.

- *Bookstores.* They're not just for the printed word anymore. Many bookstores—especially national chains—have added toys to their merchandise mix in recent years. That's true most clearly during the holiday season, but toy offerings can be found year-round. Most of the toys are licensed merchandise related to book titles. In addition, some bookstores try to stock "brainy" games that appeal to readers.
- *Pharmacies.* Many larger locations will carry a toy aisle. The selection is limited, but often the prices are quite low. In the aisles of your local drug store you are most likely to find craft and art supplies, miniature vehicles, and seasonal items, such as squirt toys in summer and Christmas-themed toys in December.
- *Technology retailers.* Amid the newest hardware, you can find technology-related toys and games. These stores are most likely to stock the current versions of desktop and handheld games. Keep in mind that their prices may not be as competitive. And although tech store staffers may know technology, they're likely to be

less informed when it comes to what is appropriate and fun for kids.

- **Video stores.** No great mystery here. Video stores sell videos, which have their place in a varied toy collection. Video stores do offer the best selection in viewed entertainment. The downside: it's likely to be at full price. Also, keep in mind that many video retailers do not accept returns on opened merchandise. Find out the store's return policy before you pay.

Step Four: Shopping for a "Hot" Toy

You asked the child in your life what he wants for a birthday or holiday gift. And wouldn't you know it? He wants the item everyone wants. The one that's so heavily promoted even you've heard of it. The one that has its image plastered on every magazine, television show, and commercial in your child's world. The one toy nobody can find. What can you do? Fortunately, there are tricks to shopping for a hot toy.

- **Start early.** Look on the calendar and decide when you think would be a really early start to your shopping—then count back two weeks. Any toy in short supply will require some serious hunting, and to avoid a panic attack, you'll want to leave yourself plenty of time.
- **Don't rely on an Internet toy seller or catalogue.** It's not unheard of to order a toy, type in your credit card number, sit back all relaxed and happy that it's over—and then a week later receive notification that your item is back-ordered. When shopping for a hot toy, don't consider your mission accomplished until you hold the item in your hand.

TOY TIP

Buy a backup. Let's face it—when you're in the market for a hot toy, you run the risk of coming up empty handed. If the item is for you or another adult, well, deal with it. But if the item is for a child, you need a backup plan in motion even as you hunt for your desired item. Consider merchandise related to the toy you hope to buy. Hot toys often spawn a wide range of related merchandise, from clothing to backpacks to artwork. Although that may not be quite what the child in your life had in mind, it may buy you some time while you attempt to acquire the real deal.

- *Quiz the store managers.* Often, toy shortages are not exactly accidental. Some are calculated to build interest and desire for a particular product. Certainly, a brand-new company might truly have miscalculated and produced too few of an item. But a major toy maker has resources to keep pace with demand. Cozy up to your local store manager and see if you can get a handle on when additional shipments, if any, might be coming in.

For early birds: How can you tell if a toy is going to be "hot"? It's not an easy task. There are well-paid toy consultants and marketing departments hoping to make that very call. But there are some signs when a toy is headed for "hot" status. For example, is the toy connected to a popular movie or television show? That will increase its airtime and help promote its status as a must-have. Has a popular celebrity—say, a talk show host or actor—taken particular interest in the toy? That can create a surge of consumer interest. Has it appeared on the cover of a major catalogue? There's nothing like a cover pic to generate demand. If your favorite department store, discount chain, or general merchandise store is featuring your toy of choice, it's gaining steam.

If you see a toy on your list fitting these criteria, buy sooner rather than later. You can always return a toy, but it's much harder to secure one after it has reached must-have status.

Step Five: Snagging a Bargain

Shopping for toys on a budget is easy if you know where to look. The key is preparation. The more you know, the better you'll be able to navigate the retail waters without racking up a huge credit card bill.

Here are where the deals are:

- *Seasonal toy stores.* These are the "now you see them, now you don't" of the toy retailing industry. They pop up in temporarily vacant mall storefronts or on table-tops in the common areas. In most cases, they are around only from Thanksgiving to Christmas. When it comes to low prices, these shops are king. Often they are selling closeout or liquidated merchandise at bargain-basement prices. The catch is obvious: there's no service whatsoever at these stores. What you see (and what you can reach yourself) is what you get. And nothing is returnable. After all, the store won't even be there after New Year's. But for rock-bottom prices, they can't be beat.

TOY TIP

Watch out for the hidden costs of toy shopping. They lurk where you least expect them. Online, they are shipping charges. Often they are not displayed until the final clicks of the sale. Shopping without a list is another way to bleed money during a toy-shopping trip. If you don't know what you want, wandering in the aisles just leaves you vulnerable to the marketing messages of the toy makers. You're much more likely to end up with toys you don't want or can't afford. Then there are the panic toys. These are the toys you buy because you're afraid you're not going to be able to find what you really want. The only good way to guard against panic toy buying is to start early enough so that you feel as though you have plenty of time. It's not easy, that's true. But it will save you cash in the long run.

- ***Free toys.*** Keep your eye out for promotions during the holiday season that offer a free toy when you purchase a certain dollar amount. Often these are appealing classic toys—a teddy bear or a coloring set. By paying attention to the promotional trends, you can pick up extras that will go a long way toward fulfilling your list. Keep in mind—it's only a bargain if the free toy is age appropriate for the child on your list. If not, it's just a gimmick.

- *Price wars.* Competition for toy sales is fierce. It's hand-to-hand combat among the discount stores, category killers, and specialty toy chains. With all the different types of store vying for your toy dollar, it's common to see price wars break out during the holiday shopping season. Watch for them especially at the very start of the season and in the last week. Keep your eye on advertised prices in newspaper circulars. Store websites may also register any price changes.

- *One-stop shopping.* Stores that sell toys plus other merchandise are eager to attract your overall business. As a result, they may offer discounts if you purchase a certain large dollar amount. Factor this in when deciding where and how you'll shop. If you can work your toy purchases in with the rest of your holiday list at one store, you may find a large discount as a bonus.

Step Six: Once You're Home

Phew! Home from the store. Think you're done? No, sir. The key to a successful shopping trip is proper follow-up. A few more steps now will save you a big headache on gift-giving day.

- *Inspect for damage.* There's still time to return or exchange an item if it's damaged or missing a part. It's not always easy to get a good look in the store, but once safe at home, peel back the tape and packaging and take a peek. If possible, try it out. Now's the time to find out if something is broken.

- *Scan for assembly directions and needed tools.* If the toy is going to be a complicated assembly project,

TOY TIP

File your receipts. Pick a place and keep them all together. You'll be thankful when it's return and exchange time.

---

get your tools together ahead of time and make sure you're ready for it. Look at the directions, see if they make sense, and consider consulting the toy manufacturer's website for additional tips. Set aside time for assembly, if necessary. Some toys are fun to assemble with a child; just be sure that the process will be safe and appropriate for the child. Other assembly jobs you'll want to take care of solo.

- ***Do you need batteries?***

Conclusion

The most important thing to remember is to plan before you shop. The more prepared you are for your toy-shopping experience, the less likely you are to dislike the whole thing and wind up with a toy your child ignores. Knowledge is power. It is also armor. The retailers can't overwhelm you if you know what you're doing.

WORKSHEET

A Child-by-Child Checklist

Before you hit the stores, complete a basic form for each child on your list.

Name:

Age:

Grade:

Favorite activity:

Favorite school subject:

Current favorite toy:

Latest skills acquired:

Newest skills emerging:

Fondest wish:

Toy ideas:

Tales from the Toy Tips Lab

In the early days of Toy Tips, I used to travel all over, and I would often go into local stores to observe parents buying toys. During the holiday season, I would often spot scenes of parents battling over particular toys in the aisles of the store. I once asked a woman as she walked away from one such confrontation why it was so important to her to have that toy. She told me that she'd seen the toy advertised on TV and assumed her daughter would want it. It's encounters like that one that inspired me to continue to promote Toy Tips and its mission of getting unbiased research out to parents. That mother should have more to go on than television commercials and her own hand-to-hand combat skills.

Chapter 8

Educational Toys

Educational toys are supposed to enlighten, but they can sure make a parent feel dumb. The whole category is complicated. Traditional toys are easy by comparison. With them, the only thing you need to worry about is, Is it fun? When it comes to educational toys, the bar is raised: Does it teach a skill? Is it geared to my child's age? Will it promote a love of learning? Will it give my child an edge in school? Will it give me peace of mind that I've put my child's playtime to constructive use?

There are many questions and very few answers. It's enough to make parents wonder if they're really smart enough to buy smart toys.

How did buying teaching toys get this hard? There has been an overall societal evolution. No longer is childhood simply a waiting period for adult life. In many ways, these early years are preparation for the challenges that lie ahead. Parents today, well versed in just how challenging life can be, are eager to give their children every preparation, every advantage, every tool for future success. For many parents, this means seeing that their kids get the very most out of their educational opportunities, supplemented by efforts at home. That has turned up the heat on educational toys. Parents who are eager to see that their children are the next generation of best-educated, best-prepared, most successful adults warm quickly to the notion that educational toys can help make that happen.

Truth is, though, that filling a toy box only with educational toys is a mistake. Any child's play life needs a bal-

ance of toys   some that are instructive and others that
have less lofty goals—to promote the overall growth and
intellectual development of the child. Toy boxes should
not be mere extensions of a classroom experience, but
rather should be filled with a good selection of toys that
will enhance and magnify what goes on in the more traditional educational space. The key is to strike a balance.

Picking an appropriate educational toy requires a bit
of advanced study. The key elements to making smart
choices among educational toys: know your child's age and
stage; know the manufacturer and its credentials; and understand your own role in the success of educational toys.

Age-and-Stage Guide to Educational Toys

When is your child ready for a particular educational toy?
It pays to keep in mind not only the child's intellectual
strengths but also his or her chronological age. Understanding how these factors work together is what will help
you come up with the appropriate toy choice.

Infants

What constitutes an educational toy for an infant? Well,
pretty much everything. At this stage, any sensory experience is educational. When baby is new to the world,
every sight, sound, and touch is a learning moment. It's
fine to buy toys that are designed to be educational for a
baby. But it's not necessary. Any toy that is safe and properly designed for an infant will be a teaching toy. Keep in
mind that there is so much to be learned that toys are
simply part of the broad spectrum of new experiences for
a baby. When you are tiny, things like sunlight and Daddy's

hat and rain on the windows are all educational. Toys are part of that cast of teaching characters.

Where to Buy?   Because just about anything offers a baby new experiences, you can take your pick of retail formats. Any store can offer you a fine educational toy for a young infant. Just be sure the toy is designed for a baby that young. It should meet appropriate safety standards, which means it must be made of nontoxic materials and be free of loose or small objects that can present a choking hazard. Stick to stores you know and trust to carry safe products. Avoid garage sales. Although they may seem like a low-cost way to pick up baby toys, hand-me-downs can be damaged in a way that can present dangers to your own child. You're better off buying retail. If you do receive hand-me-downs in gently used condition, thoroughly inspect and properly clean the items before use.

Word to the Wise   This is a time of some anxiety for parents, who are often carefully watching baby for the acquisition of certain skills to be reassured that she is "on track" or, even better, "ahead of schedule." This is a natural parental state, but it's one that toy makers have cashed in on with a vengeance. In recent years, the market has been flooded with educational toys and videos aimed at the tiniest of tykes. There are videos, specially designed mobiles, and infant toys that play classical music. All are marketed with the implication that they will help your baby's intellectual development. There is no evidence that toys that play classical music will make your child smarter than toys that play other types of music. So if you like these toys and they appeal to you and they encourage you to interact with your baby, great. But they are not going to significantly

TOY TIP

An important intellectual milestone in a young
baby's life is the learning of object permanence—the
concept that something still exists even if it is out
of view. That means games like peekaboo are highly
educational. Use your imagination: play with your
hands, baby's favorite blanket or toy, or a chair or
curtain. Although it may seem that you're just sharing a moment of giggles with your little one, in fact
you're engaging in a key educational experience.

alter your baby's acquisition of early skills, such as sitting,
talking, reaching, or grasping. These are all developmental
and neurologically programmed. You're not going to rewire
your baby's brain with an educational toy.

Older Babies

When baby sits up, at around six months or so, it's time for
a new set of educational toys. What to look for at this age?
Toys that encourage reaching, grasping, stacking, and sorting are all great educational stimulators. This is still a time
when learning is centered around motor skills—academics will come later. The learning process at this age is very
much focused on mastery of movement.

Where to Buy?   Traditional toy departments—be they
discount stores, category killers, or department stores—
make fertile shopping ground. The selection of brand-name

educational toys for older babies is best at these larger chains. Don't worry about finding a store that carries the latest wares. After all, it's new to your little one, so a classic toy will make just as big an impression. Some online stores are also good sources of brand-name educational toys for babies, but be sure to shop from a website you trust. It's easy to set up a fly-by-night shop on the Web and disappear from view soon after.

Word to the Wise   It pays to understand what educational toys can and cannot be expected to do. They are unlikely to produce a skill that isn't yet emerging. They are often quite good at encouraging baby to try out and practice a new skill. Take walking, for example. If your baby has shown zero signs of wanting to get up and walk, there's not a toy on the market that will magically produce walking. However, if your child is close—if he's pulling up, cruising holding onto the furniture, trying to stand alone— then a toy that encourages walking can be a great fit. In this case, instead of looking to the toy to produce the skill, you are asking it to magnify and help develop the skill. And that, a toy can do.

Resist the urge to follow the voice in your head that says, "Oh, my child is so bright, I'll just buy this toy that's a step up, and it'll encourage him to be more advanced." Doing that may actually be dangerous. First, toys that are designed for older children can be hazardous in the hands of a younger child. They may have small parts that are choking hazards. They may pinch little fingers or be too heavy to be safely handled by smaller hands. Second, a toy that is out of range is a waste of your money. If your child can't master it, he or she may simply ignore it. Better to spend your effort and resources on toys that your child can appreciate and benefit from right now.

TOY TIP

Read regularly to your baby. Certainly, it will be years before your child can read alone. But at this stage, you are teaching critical education skills: a love of books and an association of reading with a warm and joyful experience. As your child moves into academics, this early foundation in reading appreciation will pay off. A child that already loves books will be eager to learn to read when the time comes.

Toddlers

What's an educational toy for a toddler? At this age, education is made up of learning new motor skills and increasingly intellectual pursuits. This is a good age to begin memory games. Basic card games with images rather than numbers or words make a good choice. Be sure the materials are made for the heavy handling of a toddler. Also, this is an age when a child learns the basics of cause and effect, so toys that react to a child's push, pull, or other action will be useful. Look for toys that use these skills in age-appropriate ways. For example, a cause-and-effect toy that a toddler can handle and operate with minimal adult assistance is a good choice—don't expect the toddler to sit and watch you operate the toy. That's boring.

Where to Buy? Major chains are a good bet for toddler education toys. You can also hit the specialty stores for more unique and higher-quality items, but be prepared for higher prices.

TOY TIP

Toddlers are natural explorers, and this tremendous curiosity can be a huge benefit when it comes to classroom education. So foster your toddler's desire to learn and understand by pursuing supervised exploration trips. Open up the cabinet in the kitchen that contains the pots and pans, and explore together. Go on a hunt for interesting flora and fauna in the garden. Help your child look for a particular toy or book in his room. What are you teaching? The skills of a future explorer.

Word to the Wise   How can you get your toddler interested in educational toys? Get a little help from his make-believe friends. Many toddlers are passionate about the licensed characters they see on television, on their videos, and in their favorite bedtime stories. You can leverage a toddler's knowledge of these characters to sustain his or her interest in an educational toy. A memory game that features the faces of favorite characters will be that much more interesting to your toddler. Just because they're television characters doesn't mean they can't have an educational purpose. Be sure to pick a character appropriate for your child's age.

Preschool

Finally, the moment all anxious parents have been waiting for: the age of early academics. At this stage, educational toys begin to look more, well, educational. They begin to

incorporate the building blocks of what will eventually become classroom curriculum. Educational toys for this age
group feature letters and numbers and other more advanced concepts such as under, over, in, and beside. Look
for toys that teach early counting or encourage a child to
put letters together. Computer games can be an educational asset at this stage. As your preschooler begins to
master the art of point-and-click, games designed to teach
basic letter and number skills can be very popular. There
are also a host of Internet sites designed for this age
group. Be sure to surf them yourself first, to determine
whether the content is age appropriate and to scan for any
ads or marketing messages on the site.

Where to Buy?   For this age group, new retail categories join your shopping list. Not only chain stores and
specialty shops are good picks; now stores with a heavier
focus on technology also play a role. Retailers that sell a
lot of computer software are likely to have a much better
selection of the latest preschool computer games than
your average toy store. Be sure to cruise their aisles as
well. Also, online stores can be a good source of software.
Buy from an online merchant you know and trust and read
the fine print to be sure you understand the return and
exchange policies.

Word to the Wise   Every parent has felt the urge to de-
clare their offspring a genius and to buy ever more advanced educational toys. Resist. Really. You can do more
harm than good. When you buy an educational toy that is
too advanced, you set yourself up for two problems. The
first is your own disappointment. Your child may not be
able to achieve what you had hoped, so you're sorry you
bought the toy, sorry you wasted your money, and sorry

TOY TIP

There are many traditional educational toys available for this age group. Look for those that combine letter and number learning with additional elements, such as music or storytelling or dance. This helps infuse the learning experience with an element of entertainment. The marriage of the two won't be lost on your preschooler, and the positive association will pay off in the classroom.

the toy has done nothing to make you feel better about your child's future. Problem number two is actually the bigger issue. When you offer an educational toy that is beyond your child's ability, you risk making the child feel like a failure. Children are quite sensitive, and it's not at all unlikely that yours will pick up on your desire to see accomplishment. When it doesn't happen, the child may simply assume he or she is at fault. Good educational toys should magnify and build on skills your child has begun to master. You need to see the signs before you can expect the toy to do its job.

School Age

Educational toys for the school-age child are those that will dovetail with what the child is learning in school. They can be vocabulary games, math puzzles, strategy games, or geography quests. They can take the form of a book, a game, a piece of software, or an activity toy. There's no reason at all to assume that an educational toy for a school-age child must be a quiet, sit-at-the-table kind of toy. Many of the better-designed educational toys for this age group will encourage a good deal of rough-and-tumble play. Learning can be engaging and fun. Educational toys can help bring that aspect of intellectual development to life.

Where to Buy?   For this age group, branch out from traditional toy stores and investigate bookstores, music stores, museum shops, and other unique retail establishments for ideas. School-age kids can spot a learning toy a mile away, so you'll want to go to some trouble to be sure the ones you buy and offer are attractive. Tying in to kids' favorite licensed characters is a good way to snag their attention. So is bringing them on a shopping expedition. Just as a child who helps prepare a dinner is more likely to try the new foods, a school-age child who has helped pick out an educational toy is more likely to embrace the choice.

Word to the Wise   Educational toys can help support your child's classroom performance, but they are not miracle workers. You can't look to a toy to vault your child to the head of the class. Also, if your child is lagging in a particular subject, a toy that teaches in that area can help, but it can't be counted on to fix the problem by itself. Do not substitute a toy for your involvement or the attention of a tutor or other outside help. Keep in mind that an educational toy can help your child master a certain subject or set of material, but it will not make your child smarter.

TOY TIP

Use your child's classroom as a springboard for choosing educational toys. If your child is learning about dinosaurs at school, consider a dinosaur model kit or a dino coloring book or a game that features prehistoric times. If the classroom studies are covering explorers, try out geography games and puzzles.

Know Your Toy Maker

It's always a good idea to know something about the manufacturer when making a toy purchase, but it's an especially crucial bit of knowledge when you're in the market for educational toys. Toy making is an ever-changing business. There are a lot of old standbys still out there, but many more new companies burst on the scene each year. In the educational toy category, newcomers are common. In fact, they are often the companies getting the most attention from retailers and the press. These toys can create a great deal of excitement among consumers eager to snap up a great innovation in fun learning. Whether you're buying from an established company or a newcomer, it pays to do an inventory of the company's background in educational products.

- **_Know the company._** What else does it make? A company devoted to educational toys can offer you a track record of success with previous products. If the company is primarily a doll maker but is now out with an educational game, you may want to do some more investigation to see if the product is right for you.

- ***Know the management.*** When possible, look at the résumés of the company officials. What's the background of the person who presents you with this educational toy? Is the toy's creator a teacher? A parent? A sales executive? All have different skill sets that will lead them to create different kinds of toys with different kinds of educational goals. How much research went into the creation of the toy? Sometimes that information isn't readily available, but it's worth a try. Check out the company website or press coverage of the firm to see if you can get an idea.

- ***Ask the teachers.*** Don't be shy about asking teachers about educational toys. Teachers don't see them as competition. In fact, many teachers incorporate educational toys, especially group games and projects, into their classroom work. So they are likely to be quite knowledgeable when it comes to the latest and greatest educational toys.

Technology and Educational Toys

Not all educational toys are high-tech; not all tech toys are educational. There's a broad misconception about technology toys, namely that because they embrace the latest in technology, they are educational. Not so at all. Just because the toy needs batteries—or a power source or a wireless network—does not necessarily qualify it as an educational toy.

Some tech toys *are* educational. These are toys that teach a topic, hone a skill, encourage development of a

TOY TIP

Even though many technology toys are designed for individual play, sit with your child and play when first introducing an educational technology toy. It may require some demonstration on your part. Sit together, whether it's at the computer or on the playroom floor, to figure out the new toy together. That way you can be sure the educational value of the toy is coming through.

desired activity. Be aware that sales clerks at technology stores will be more well versed in the hardware and technical features than in the educational value of various toys, so you may need to do some outside research to find out if a tech toy has true teaching potential. Look online or consider asking a teacher for advice.

On the flip side, some utterly tech-free toys can be tremendous teachers. A power source doesn't transform a toy into a teacher. Don't worry that because you've passed up a computer chip, you've bypassed the educational aspects of a toy.

Educational Videos

These are tough to judge. If they're not entertaining, they're useless. No child will voluntarily sit in front of a dull instructional video. At the same time, you have to wonder: If they're all about entertainment, are they really teaching? You might be just as well off with regular TV. What can you do to pick good educational videos?

- *Combine teaching with popular characters.* Favorite faces from TV shows and other entertainment properties are a good way to introduce educational concepts while retaining a small child's attention.
- *Be skeptical of educational videos for babies.* There's a growing number of videos marketed to parents of infants. The concept behind them is that specially created videos will enhance a baby's development. But there's little research to show that the videos rise above the entertainment level and actually promote learning. Babies learn from everything around them. Videos are no more suited to teaching than other baby toys. On the downside, they may create a false sense of security in the parent. If you've left the baby watching a video, don't be lulled into the idea that he or she is learning. You've still put the baby in front of the television set.

The Parental Factor

Parents are often frustrated by what they perceive as the failure of the educational toys they buy. It seems the child didn't learn the skills the parent had hoped to see. But the breakdown is often not with the toys. Educational toys require an outside ingredient critical to their success. It isn't batteries. It's parental involvement.

When you bring out an educational toy, show enthusiasm for it. Explore it with your child. Learn together how it works and make the play and learning a shared experience. If you send your child off to his or her room with an educational toy and expect that to do the trick, you may be disappointed. But if you invest the time and attention to engage your child with the toy, you'll be more likely to see the learning results you hope for.

Is This Educational? A Guide by Toy Type

Every toy category includes toys that can be educational. Some are designed that way. Others are learning toys if you use them the right way. What follows is a guide, arranged by toy type, to give you some ideas.

Stuffed Toys

- *Educational value:* promotes the expansion of the emotional IQ. They foster a sense of attachment and security.
- *Examples:* anything plush and huggable. It can be a classic teddy bear, a friendly monster of TV fame, or a big red puppy.
- *Best for:* toddlers. This is the age when they are learning the skills of managing emotional attachment. A favorite stuffed animal can help smooth the transition from infant dependency on mom and dad to the more independent play of early childhood.

Construction Toys

- *Educational value:* construction toys teach spatial relationships, fine motor skills, planning and strategy, and perseverance.
- *Examples:* basic building blocks, plastic connector sets, complex model replicas.
- *Best for:* preschool and up. Be sure you pick a construction toy that is in tune with the child's current fine motor skills. These sets are no fun if you can't put them together yourself.

Dolls

- *Educational value:* there are so many kinds of dolls that to corral them into one teaching theme would be impossible. Dolls can teach everything from the fine motor skills of dressing and undressing, to empathy and caring, to independent play skills.
- *Examples:* baby dolls, collectible dolls, culturally diverse dolls.
- *Best for:* preschool and up. Doll preferences will change with age. A younger child may gravitate to dolls that represent family members, whereas a school-age child may be more interested in dolls that depict faraway lands. Keep in mind that both boys and girls can play with dolls. Consider it part of *your* education!

Puzzles

- *Educational value:* puzzles teach fine motor skills, concentration, visual skills, and perseverance.
- *Examples:* wooden block puzzles, plastic cube and shape puzzles, traditional jigsaw puzzles.
- *Best for:* school-age children. A smaller child may like a basic wooden block puzzle, but the true nature of a "puzzle person" will likely emerge a little later in childhood.

Board Games

- *Educational value:* board games can teach counting skills, strategy, good sportsmanship, and reading skills.
- *Examples:* checkers, classic board games, advanced strategy games.

- **Best for:** preschool and up. It depends on the game you choose. There are excellent board games for children as young as age three that teach early counting skills and require no reading. There are also complex board games of strategy and risk clearly designed for school age and up. Board games are fun—and educational—for all ages.

Action Figures

- **Educational value:** they don't look much like teachers, but there *is* educational value in the little plastic guys. They can help enhance motor skills, and they encourage imaginative play. In addition, they are often connected to a detailed back story. Action figures can be a bridge to comic books and other reading material.
- **Examples:** everyone from Spider-Man to today's latest heroes.
- **Best for:** school age. A child who reads will be best able to derive the educational value of the action figure. Younger children will see it more as a straight plaything.

Activity Toys

- **Educational value:** any time a toy asks a child to create something, there's learning involved. A good activity toy will engage a child in creating an educational experience.
- **Examples:** science projects, craft projects, experiments.
- **Best for:** preschool and up. School-age children will be able to engage with an activity toy relatively independently; preschoolers will require closer supervision. Be

sure you choose a toy that uses products safe for a child.

Talking Toys

- *Educational value:* these toys encourage children to react to auditory cues. This is an important skill to have when a child first enters a school or preschool environment. These toys help develop necessary listening skills as well as early speech skills.
- *Examples:* tape recorders, interactive plush toys, child-size keyboard toys.
- *Best for:* older infants and up. These toys are designed for a broad spectrum of ages. Look for a toy that will magnify and build on a skill your child already has.

Conclusion

Perhaps the most important thing to remember about educational toys is that in the end, they are toys. They are not replacements for traditional academics or parental involvement. Use educational toys to find fun and engaging ways to foster a love of learning in your child, but remember to involve yourself as well in this kind of play. Your interest and enthusiasm for education is what will have the most impact on your child's ultimate academic success

WORKSHEET

Match the Toy with the School Subject

Do you know which toys support which academic skills? Test your knowledge in this quiz.

School Subject	Teaching Toy
1. Reading	A. Chess
2. Writing	B. Globes
3. Spelling	C. Trivia games
4. Geography	D. Videos
5. History	E. Telescope
6. Art	F. Karaoke
7. Science	G. Chalkboard
8. Foreign language	H. Hangman
9. Math	I. Finger paint
10. Music	J. Phonics toys

Answers:

1J   2G   3H   4B   5C   6I   7E   8D   9A   10F

Tales from the Toy Tips Lab

In my experience, the best way to teach a child a skill is to have a favorite adult demonstrate. Even better, have a favorite adult show a passion for the task. My father plays the guitar. Since he was an infant, my son watched and listened to his grandfather play. He began to imitate him on his own "kiddie guitar." More than music class or instruction, just seeing his grandfather show interest and enthusiasm for a task was enough to inspire him to try.

Chapter 9

Videos and DVDs

If there is any one plaything that separates our generation from that of our children, it is the video. What was once a luxury item, even an unheard of technological wonder for parents, is a staple of today's childhood. Today, the VCR and the video library are commonplace in children's homes, their schools and libraries—virtually anyplace they spend time. Video watching is as common as any other leisure activity for today's child.

Videos are omnipresent, the product of an enormous industry in a constant state of activity, serving up everything from entertainment to education to brainless hogwash. There is no shortage of producers of children's video. Some of it is high-quality entertainment produced by some of the best-trained visual artists in Hollywood. Some of it is hastily produced in someone's basement and shipped out directly to the discount bin in chain stores. From television shows to major motion pictures to original story lines, the video industry is positively awash in choices for parents.

And so you face a prickly decision: Should I let my child watch videos? If I do, which ones should I pick? This chapter addresses the video issues of the modern parent.

Videos: Yea or Nay?

Like any plaything, videos have their pros and cons. Some are excellent, some are lousy, all require some parental supervision to be of maximum play value. There are plenty of good reasons to ban video watching altogether. After all, there are other more entertaining, educational, and healthy activities a child can pursue. But in this day and age, it's likely a child will watch videos for at least some portion of time. So, as a parent, you need to understand the pros and cons and make smart rules and choices for your child.

Video Pros

- *Videos are entertaining.* Let's face it, a good video is fun. And there's nothing wrong with that, after all. In a day filled with school, homework, chores, and sports, an entertaining video is a welcome addition to the lineup.
- *Videos can teach.* Often, when a parent is having trouble teaching a particular concept, from potty training to stranger danger to how to be a good friend, videos can be a great source of support and information. A well-chosen video can also be used to support classroom work—enhancing academic skills, such as prereading, or social skills, such as sharing and telling the truth.
- *Videos hold a child's attention.* If you're trying to get dinner on the table or an older child settled into a homework assignment, or if five minutes of uninterrupted conversation with your spouse sounds nice, a video can do the trick.
- *Videos span age groups.* When you've got more than one child to entertain and they aren't the same age, often a video can bridge the gap. Although a teen probably won't appreciate toddler fare, many entertainment videos, such as feature-length films, can appeal to a variety of ages.

Video Cons

- *Videos are passive.* A toy is something a child interacts with. Most videos ask only that the child be an audience.
- *Videos can have inappropriate content.* This can range from words or language you find offensive to scenes of violence or intimacy you're not ready to show your child. It's sometimes hard to tell from the box that the video contains scenes you as a parent won't like.
- *Videos can be overused.* It's fine to pop in a video for the occasional moment. But making it a constant virtual babysitter can be problematic. This is also an issue to raise with babysitters and teachers.
- *Videos = couch potato-ism.* Kids in our society today get too little exercise. One of the contributors to that problem is the vast availability of children's videos. It becomes easy, even preferable, to plop down on the sofa for half an hour of entertainment rather than see who's around for a game of tag or other outdoor activity.

Clearly there are two sides to the video argument. Any decisions you make have to be sensible for the child and the family. Decide how much time you are willing to allocate to video watching and make this an explicit family rule. Kids are less likely to whine, complain, or beg if the rule is clear and consistent. So for a small child, researchers say that thirty minutes in a day is plenty. Be sure to make this rule clear to other adults who may care for the child, such as an older sibling, relative, or babysitter.

Remember as you make and enforce your video time limits that videos count as television time. So if you're setting a tube time limit, you'll want to factor in any video time as well. Although you can control the content during video time—and that's a good thing—this does not take the activity significantly above ordinary time spent watching television. The activity is the same—sitting and watching— even though the content may be more to your liking. So don't be lulled into thinking that if your child is watching videos—even the educational variety—he or she is not taking in TV time. It's still television, no matter what's on.

How to Choose a Great Video

Picking a great video is a team effort. There's you, and then there's some outside information that by itself is somewhat useless but that when combined with your good judgment can lead you to smart video choices.

The Parental Part

First, read the box. You won't get much from it, but it's a start. Next, screen the video yourself. Yes, yes, that takes time, and you are pressed for time, but it's worth it. Once you are familiar with a particular series or production label, you may be able to make a choice without pre-screening the video in full. But making a decision based on the text on the box and the advice from the video store clerk is hardly foolproof.

When screening, here's what to look for:

- *Character message.* Ask yourself these questions as you watch: What is each of the characters projecting? What sorts of qualities do they have? How do they handle the various twists in the story line? How would you feel if your child decided to act out one of these char-acters? Not all the characters have to be "good guys." After all, there's plenty of room in a child's imagination for heroes and villains. But watch the characters in gen-eral to get a sense of who they are and what they're about.

- **Values.** Does the story line or message fit in generally with your overall family values? Do the characters do or say things that you would not consider appropriate for your child? For some families, this is an issue of violent content. Others look at the moral judgments embedded in the story line. Do the characters lie or steal? Are there consequences for bad behavior?

- **Age appropriateness.** Children will often copy and act out what they see in videos. So what are the char-acters in this video doing? Are they on a treasure hunt? Are they going to school or to the zoo or on a picnic? Are they involved in a fantasy? Dealing with peer pres-sure? Different topics will appeal to and be appropriate for different age groups.

- **Dialogue.** How do the characters in this video talk to one another? One of the great complaints of the video age is that children will often mimic the dialogue they hear in their favorite entertainment. Are the characters in this video speaking in such a way that you would not be offended or embarrassed to hear their dialogue com-ing out of your child's mouth?

Industry 411

In addition to your own screening, there are some outside ratings systems that can help you make decisions. Do not rely on these letter "grades" to make your final call—your own opinion of what makes a fine family movie may differ greatly from the opinion of your average Hollywood producer. But the ratings do offer some broad guidelines for video choices.

For Videos Based on Motion Pictures   The Motion Picture Association of America (MPAA) is a good place to start. The trade group has developed a well-known rating system designed to educate consumers about a movie's content. Although these ratings are just the opinion of this one organization, they are a solid first step in evaluating entertainment options.

G: for general audiences. This is content the MPAA has deemed appropriate for all ages. That means it won't contain strong content such as sex or violence. However, a G rating does not mean that it is automatically appropriate for your child. Keep in mind, for example, that many very popular Disney movies depict the death of a parent or other intense subjects. Although they may not be displayed graphically, the themes are still present, and you as a parent will need to decide when and how your child will see these stories.

PG: some content in the story may not be suitable for children. You'll need to know what that piece of content is and decide whether or not it meets the suitability requirements for your child. It may be something like sexual innuendo or coarse language. Or it may be a scene of violence. Important to note: do not assume all cartoons carry a G rating. It is quite common to find animated videos today that are intended for older audiences.

PG-13: this is a relatively new rating in the system. It was added in response to the reality that not all children have the same entertainment tastes. A child of three clearly has different needs than a child of fourteen. This rating makes a more direct distinction between older and younger children. A PG-13 video is likely to have scenes that include sexual innuendo, violence, or illegal activity.

R and NC-17: both ratings signify content intended solely for adults.

For Videos Based on Television Content   These ratings developed by the TV Parental Guidelines Board appear on the televised content as it airs on broadcast or cable, as well as on the box of the video version. The ratings are voluntary and are added by broadcast and cable television networks.

TVY: all children. This program is designed to be appropriate for all children. Whether it is a cartoon or a live-action show, it contains core elements and themes that are designed specifically for audiences ages two to six. A video with this rating is not supposed to be scary.

TVY7: older children. The content in these videos will have been designed for children, but may be most suitable for kids who have mastered the distinction between make-believe and reality. Content may include scenes of fantasy or comedic violence, and it's possible a child under seven would find it frightening.

TVY7FV: a video designed for children seven and up, with a bit more intensity. Scenes of fantasy violence (FV) may be more combative than those that do not carry an FV designation. Parents will need to decide whether or not this content is suitable for their school-age children.

TVG: although many parents would consider this type of video suitable for all ages, it is not designed specifically for children. A video with this rating will contain little or no violence, no strong language, and little or no sexual dialogue or situations.

TVPG: this video may contain content that parents consider unsuitable for younger children. It may be a video that parents will want to watch with their children, to offer any explanation or context for the content. The theme of the video itself may be the reason for the suggested additional parental guidance, or there may be additional elements signified by additional letter ratings. The V rating indicates moderate violence; an S signifies some sexual situations; L indicates the use of coarse language; D flags the use of suggestive dialogue. These additional letters may give parents a clue as to why the video holds a TVPG rating. So if you see a TVPGD rating, you can assume the video has content that may be unsuitable for young children because of the use of sexually suggestive dialogue.

TV14: this is a video that will contain one or more of the following: intense violence (sometimes signified by an additional letter rating of V); intense sexual situations (S); strong, coarse language (L); or intensely suggestive dialogue (D). Parents are advised not to let their children under fourteen years old watch this video unattended.

TVMA: this video is designed for mature audiences—that's viewers over seventeen. It may contain graphic violence or explicit sexual activity.

Rating Educational Videos

In this category, you'll have to act as your own ratings system. Here's how to know if the video your child is watching is actually educational:

- ***Does it explicitly teach a skill?*** Educational videos should not be overly subtle. This is a young audience with a short attention span. Look for content that is clear and direct and that makes its teaching point openly. That's especially important for educational videos aimed at young children. Older kids may be better able to divine an educational message buried in a detailed story line, but toddlers and preschoolers need the direct approach. Be sure your educational video makes its point clearly.

- ***Is your child repeating the educational messages away from the TV?*** For example, is he or she recognizing the shapes and letters from the video in other situations, such as at preschool or out in the park? This is a good indication that the video is doing its job—presenting the information in such a way that the child can then apply it outside of the video-watching time.

- ***Does it generate additional parent-child interaction?*** Sometimes a great educational video opens a door to a broader educational process. Some of the most successful educational videos are those that take on one topic and hammer it home. If you're working on potty training or learning to share or coping with fears about the doctor or dentist, a video on this topic may give you just the boost you need to get an individual conversation going with your child.

How to Be a Savvy Video Shopper

Having tackled the complex educational and sociological topics of video content, now comes the really hard part: how to acquire videos without losing your shirt. It can be a great big black hole down which you pour cash, thinking you're making great investments in childhood entertainment. Instead, you end up with shelves of unused tapes that gather dust and taunt you with their inactive status.

Shopping for videos is not easy, and retailers don't help you. Many stores will not allow you to return a video that's been opened, so if you are a smart parent and you screen a video, you are often out of luck when you want your money back. Still, you have options:

- *The public library.* Many major branches of public libraries have ample video collections for checkout. This is a great way to screen videos before you show them to your child, or to view one that you're thinking of buying as a gift. Combine your video excursions with a trip to the reading section as well.
- *Video stores.* They are good sources for popular videos. Scan your neighborhood for the store with the best children's section. Talk with your child about the videos you will choose before you get to the store. If possible, discuss a first, second, and third choice, to protect against out-of-stock disappointments. By setting some parameters before you enter the store, you are less likely to experience an in-store tantrum when your child wants to rent a video you don't approve of.
- *Online stores.* Many new businesses have sprung up on the Internet that allow consumers to rent videos or DVDs online. This can be a great option for parents. It saves time because you don't have to schlep to the video store, and often these online clubs are designed so that you can keep a title for a while without incurring late charges. That's a huge benefit for parents

whose children watch a favorite video multiple times before sending it back to the store.

- **_Discount stores._** Not much on selection, but you can't beat the prices. These stores are most likely to stock the best-selling titles—videos based on major motion pictures or developed from popular televised characters.
- **_Toy chains._** Big-box toy stores have increased their interest in the video business in recent years and are more likely to carry a good selection of children's videos. Check the return policy: many will not let you return a video that's been opened.

Where Videos Come From—and Why You Should Care

Videos come from a variety of entertainment sources, and often their origins can help you decide when and why they're appropriate for your child. Different video production sources have different goals and different audiences in mind for their products.

Movie Studios

Hollywood makes movies. Often these movies wind up in video form, but in most cases, the primary viewing is meant for the big screen. What does that mean? It means they really didn't make these products with very small children in mind. Toddlers just aren't big moviegoers. Entertainment created for theatrical release is often designed to have broad appeal. The more people, the more tickets, the better the box office performance. That means a major

TOY TIP

For a special treat, pick out your favorite full-length feature, make some popcorn, and gather the family for movie night. It's a great family tradition and one that can build strong ties and fond memories among family members. You can extend the invitation to grandparents and other relatives. You can allow older children to invite a pal. Dim the lights and make it a true entertainment event.

motion picture, even one made for children, is likely to try to span the broadest possible age range.

How can you use this information? Expect a video that comes originally from a movie to appeal primarily to older children. These films have longer, more involved stories. Very young children may lack the interest or the attention span to sit down and watch a full-length movie. Also, it's not unusual for the visual effects to be quite intense. That's the nature of Hollywood. So you'll want to be careful and screen for scenes that may be scary or overly intense for young children.

The length of major motion pictures causes another problem. If you've got a time limit on video watching—say, thirty minutes—popping a theatrical movie into the VCR is somewhat unfair. There's no way the kids get to see it all at once, and small children really can't keep a story line in their heads long enough to watch a movie over a week's time. Keep these for special family movie nights or other special occasions.

Television

Network and cable television is an unending source of material for the video industry. The televised content itself is often available in video form. A long-running animated or live-action series may put out previous seasons on video. Or television properties may license their wares to companies that make direct-to-video products featuring the popular characters.

What does this mean to you? Videos from television can offer many benefits. They depict characters your child already knows, and therefore you're much more likely to get a positive response from your young viewer. Also, many of the creators of educational television programs have invested heavily in video. So if you're anxious to expose your child to educational videos but you're concerned he or she

 TOY TIP

Television's greatest contribution to the video industry is a wide range of videos that teach and support educational themes. Build your home collection around these teaching tools and forgo stocking up on the ordinary cartoons. That way, when the kids want a video to wind down, the offerings you have on hand have at least a small amount of benefit. From public television to cable shows designed to teach reading and foreign language skills, the assortment is wide. Keep a keen eye out for the more educationally oriented of the pack.

might reject the notion, a video connected to a popular television show may aid the transition.

Another plus: videos based on television are often packaged in the traditional television segments of thirty minutes. For parents with a time limit, the thirty-minute video works nicely. When the video is over, the TV goes off. No arguments about what time it is and five more minutes please.

Direct-to-Video

Hollywood and networks may get all the ink, but there's a vast selection of video product that is completely independent and has no connection whatsoever to the established entertainment monsters. That's both the good news and the bad news for parents. On the one hand, it's good, because it means there's entertainment out there for your child that has not been run through the official fantasy machine of entertainment conglomerates. On the other hand, this is uncharted space. It's very difficult to know which of these independent videos are worthwhile for your child, and there's not a lot of good detailed information to help you sort through the selection.

Here's what to do:

- *Talk to teachers.* And librarians. And other professionals who work regularly with children. They may have a line on video products that are off the beaten path but wonderful for kids.
- *Talk to other parents.* Although not all families have the same values and standards, they can still be a good point of initial recommendations for good videos.

TOY TIP

Use the direct-to-video category to branch out and try some new formats. If your child is used to animated videos, try some live action. Look for videos that introduce your child to new music, new cultures, or new forms of entertainment. Sure, these don't feature the characters your child knows by heart, but it's fine—even beneficial—to expand your child's cast of entertainment characters. Leverage this video category to expand your child's horizons.

- **Read reviews.** Again, not all reviewers will share your sensibilities, but they can often tip you off to new entertainment choices on the market.

VHS or DVD?

If you've already got one type of player in the household, don't rush out and buy the other. There's no reason your child can't share the family technology. That said, there are pros and cons to each format.

- **VHS.** Currently, the selection of children's entertainment is quite a bit larger on VHS than it is on DVD. That situation won't last. It will probably be only a few years before DVD catches up and then a few more before it eclipses the old format entirely. But because VHS came first, the VHS library is more robust.

- **_DVD._** In many ways DVD is superior to VHS, and its
  ease of use with kids is one of its advantages. There is
  no rewinding when you use a DVD. For any parent that
  has told a whiny two-year-old to wait while a favorite
  video rewinds, this will be a very, very popular feature.
  Also, DVDs hold up better under heavy use. Young children are very hard on their favorite entertainment: they
  want to watch it over and over and over again. Discs
  handle this treatment better than tapes. Finally, any
  adult who has watched a movie on DVD knows that the
  format lends itself to nifty extras. This is true for children's DVDs as well. DVD makers will often add on a
  computer game or other bonus track.

  Another format issue: when buying a DVD, keep in
mind that the industry has yet to establish fully compati-
ble global standards. So it's possible to buy a DVD in Eu-
rope that won't play on a U.S. machine, and vice versa. If
you (or your gift) will be crossing international datelines,
be sure the DVD packaging carries a global label so that it
can be played in its new home.

And Now, a Word from Our Sponsor

Sometimes parents will opt for a video over a television
program because they think it shields the child from commercial messages. Sadly, that's a myth. Commercial messages have infiltrated the video library. Although they may
not take the form of familiar thirty-second ad spots,
they're there. Here are some examples:

- **_Movie tie-ins._** Often a video of a major motion picture
  will include ads at the beginning of the tape for mer-

chandise related to the movie or other upcoming features from the same production company.

- ***TV spinoffs.*** Videos that feature TV characters will often feature ads that hawk merchandise and movie spinoffs.
- ***Public television.*** Even educational videos are not commercial free. Videos that feature beloved educational characters will also feature spots promoting other videos for sale.

You can fast-forward through these images, although that requires a certain quickness of thumb. Or you can be prepared for your children to learn these ads by heart, just as they do the primary content of the video they love.

Conclusion

Video entertainment is a big part of children's lives today, so don't just sit back and become part of the audience. The role of the parent is to jump in and sort through the enormous variety of merchandise offered and help make some sense of the selection. Videos can be useful and entertaining additions to a child's life. But don't count on the child to know the good videos from the bad. That job falls to you.

WORKSHEET

The Ratings Game

Think you know your family classics from your teen fare? Maybe, maybe not. Test your knowledge by assigning these favorites an MPAA rating. You may be surprised.

1. *The Wizard of Oz*
2. *E.T.*
3. *The Sound of Music*
4. *Treasure Island*
5. *Snow White and the Seven Dwarfs*
6. *Batman*
7. *Big*
8. *Kindergarten Cop*
9. *The Black Stallion*
10. *Willy Wonka and the Chocolate Factory*

Answers:

1G   2PG   3Unrated   4PG   5G   6PG-13   7PG   8PG-13   9G   10G

Tales from the Toy Tips Lab

Children are far more affected by media images than we realize. Even when we are not directly exposing them to a particular medium, they often absorb it anyway. I realized this when I toy-tested a Flintstones playset with preschoolers, which was developed by a toy company in advance of the live-action Flintstones movie. The children were too young to have seen the original cartoon. So at first they took to the toys and made up their own scenarios. They called them "Rock People." Later, after publicity for the movie had begun, I observed the children playing with the toys and using the character names—Fred, Barney, and so on. Finally, after the movie had been in theaters, I noticed them acting out actual scenes with the toys. Not all these children had seen the movie. The mere fact that the movie existed influenced their play.

Chapter 10

Family Toys

Toys are for children, right?

Yes and no. Certainly, toys are primarily for youngsters. But that needn't be an unbreakable rule. Smart grown-ups know you're never too old to have fun, and some toys—properly chosen—can enter a specialized play category: family toys. Not every toy can be a family toy. It takes a particular type of plaything and a generous amount of parental preparation to make a fulfilling family toy. But chosen well, family toys are a true gift. They are more than just playthings; they are memory makers.

Still, attaining that specialized status is hardly child's play. Picking a great family toy is hard work. It requires good knowledge not just of the toys but of the players and the circumstances of the playtime. Making a great family toy choice is a skill. Here's what you need to know to make for memorable family playtime.

What Is a Family Toy?

Let's start off with a definition. A family toy has several key attributes:

- *Multigenerational.* Some toys are clearly for a particular age group. Rattles are for babies. Bicycles are for older children. Toys that involve physical strength may be best for teens or adults. But some toys cross the generational boundaries and make great candidates for family toys. If you can picture anyone in the family, from the youngest to the oldest, having fun with the toy, you've got a winner. If, when you imagine playing with this toy, one member of the family is either too old or too young to play, it's not for family time.

- **Group-friendly.** Most family toys are best played by the family all at the same time. It's not a hard-and-fast requirement. Some great family toys can be played in turn. But most involve the whole group at once. The toy may be designed specifically for group play, or it may be one that can be played either individually or en masse.

- **Flexible.** When play is confined to a child and a peer or two, it's easy to keep all players focused. But when you gather the family for playtime, there's going to be an added element of unpredictability: instead of peers, you've got a range of ages, play expertise, and abilities. So a great family toy must be flexible. It must be the kind of toy that can be adapted to fit a toddler mood, a visiting relative, or a cool teen.

Here's another element many family toys share: location. They are very likely already in your child's toy box. Sometimes you'll need to make a special trip to the store for a family toy purchase. But for the most part, great family toys can be adapted from your current stock of playthings. So if you've got it in your mind that you'd like to try some family playtime, don't hit the stores. Review the toys you've already got and go from there. Often, it's the planning, not the plaything, that makes the memory.

Planning Tips

A little forethought can make all the difference when it comes to family playtime. Although spontaneous family fun is wonderful, it's often not possible given the busy lives of families today. So to avoid rushed or unfulfilling play, put some mental muscle into the game.

First, consider the oldest and youngest in the group. The toy and play you pick must be accessible to both ends of your age spectrum. So a game can't be so complicated that the youngest is left out. Be aware of toys that require reading or other academic skills and be sensitive to the fact that those elements may exclude younger family members. At the same time, consider your older players. Although they may be better able to tolerate a toy that excludes them, it detracts from the full family fun. Watch for toys or games that call for physical strength, flexibility, or manual dexterity. These may not be fun for the grandparents at play. Also, some knowledge-based games may be just right for teens but far off the mark from the knowledge base of your average parent or grandparent.

Second, consider the timing of your play. There are many times to schedule family play, but the time you pick can have a significant effect on the overall enjoyment of the play. If you've got a toddler in the group, you may want to avoid the early evening—often called the witching hour by experienced parents. It's a time of day that seems to bring out the tantrum in even the happiest of toddlers. They'll do better in the morning. Choice of day is also an important timing issue. If you envision family playtime as part of a holiday gathering, consider what other events are planned for the day. You don't want to get everyone involved in a game moments before the festival meal is served. Timing is everything, even in playtime.

Finally, pave the way for flexibility. Family playtime is no fun if it deteriorates into family bickering time. To avoid that, make a point of encouraging flexibility among the players. Discuss this desired state of mind with the adults and older children who will be playing. It doesn't matter who wins or loses, it's how the family plays together. Adjust your own attitude to Flexible, and the rest of the group will be more likely to follow suit.

Picking the Toy

OK, you've planned, you've prepared, you've prepped the crowd. Now you're set to pick the toys. Here are some suggestions and their family play applications.

Board Games

Perhaps the most popular and well-known choice for family playtime is the board game. It has all the elements of a great family toy. It appeals to a wide age range, it can be played by the rules or by family whim, and it is designed for two or more players. Board games are a diverse enough category that it's not hard to find a game that can span a range of ages and interests. Not all board games require reading—if you've got a preschooler in your group, you may opt for a more visual game. Also, board games are increasingly creative. Today you can find games based on popular television shows; games that call for acting skill, teamwork, or trivia knowledge; and games that incorporate technology. Whether newly designed or classic, board games remain a smart family toy choice.

Dolls

Not all dolls make good family toys. Some are designed, appropriate, and best suited for the youngest of players. But many dolls—especially collectible dolls—span generations beautifully and can make marvelous family play memories. Dolls present more than a one-time play period.

They are a toy category that can foster a relationship between an adult and a child. The bond may develop both by collecting a particular type of doll or by amassing dolls from other lands or cultures or those representing careers, sports, or famous figures. There are endless possibilities. School-age children may be best suited to this particular form of family play, but it is a shared activity that can last for years. Early introduction to family doll play is fine, so long as an adult is careful to supervise and protect any delicate or valuable collectibles from harm. Be sure that any doll you hand a small child is safe—free of small parts that can be choking hazards.

Cars and Trains

This is a classic family toy category. Toy cars and trains are fun to collect and fun to play with. Adults are just as pumped as the kids when the switch is flipped and the train set bursts into life. Vehicle play can be anything from pushing toy cars across the kitchen floor to setting up intricate train displays around the Christmas tree. Warning: be sure to factor in the setup time. If you're hoping for some fun and family play with a large and complicated vehicle collection, consider making some preplay setup time part of the plan. It's no fun to sit around and watch one person put the fun together while everyone else waits and waits. That said, some kids enjoy being part of the setup team, so consider your family's individual tastes.

Technology Toys

Contrary to popular belief, not all technology toys are socially isolating. In fact, many tech toys make great family games. Many of the popular handheld games now have cables that can connect machines for group play. Family members can log on and engage in virtual group play. (This is a good solution for family play when family members live far apart.) Even traditional video games can be family games if everyone can take turns. Warning: technology toys are often not well suited to multigenerational play. Older players may find the technology confusing, and younger players may not be up to speed. So choose tech toys wisely.

Puzzles

This is a category that is made for family play. Even a very tough puzzle is doable if everyone pitches in. Smaller children can be set to look for particular pieces. Older kids can help in the assembly. Adults are equipped to see the bigger picture as the puzzle comes together. Because there are so many toys with bells and whistles on the market today, many families may overlook puzzle play. But these are great toys for family events.

Activity Toys

One great way to establish family play is with activity toys. Because these toys often involve the creation of an object—such as a model or other craft project—they can be played at any speed the group desires. Activity toys adapt well to the mood of the group. If everyone is in a contemplative mood, a long, leisurely, and well-planned craft project may be in order. If more action is called for, a quick session of paper airplane building followed by paper airplane play may be at hand. As with other toys, consider the age range of the group when choosing your activity toy. Activities that require significant manual dexterity may be ill suited to older and younger members of your family group. Also be sure to have all the necessary materials on hand before getting started.

Sports Toys

Like board games, sports games are classic family fun. Everything from touch football to catch qualifies. There are two key elements to great family sports play. The first is picking a game that the group can enjoy. Traditional sports are fine—rules for football, baseball, and other team sports can be adapted for family play. Consider relaxing the rules, such as by allowing as many swings as necessary to get a hit. The second important consideration is equipment. Sports equipment designed for adults may be a poor fit for children and can ruin family play in a hurry. A bat that is too heavy or a football that hurts tender fingers is no fun at all and can result in tears early in the game. Instead, opt for the softer versions of traditional sports gear if a good portion of your team is school age or younger. Older players can still enjoy the play, and younger kids won't get hurt.

Classic Toys

From train sets to board games, classic toys often are great family play choices. A key reason: the adults will remember how to play. That cuts down on the learning curve for the older participants. Also, the classic games will bring back memories for the adult players, and playing them again creates a moment to share family experiences with a younger generation. These toys are easy to pick: reach back to your own childhood for the games and toys you enjoyed and look for their modern incarnations. Some games and toys have been updated; others are just as you remember them.

Construction Toys

A building project makes an excellent family toy. Children and adults can participate in its erection, and the entire family can marvel at the finished project. The key to success with this category: choice of materials. Construction toys are designed for a range of age groups, and the secret to family fun with this toy is picking the right supplies for your builders. For projects that involve toddlers or preschoolers, opt for large plastic building blocks or others that are easily handled by tiny hands. Anything smaller or more delicate may be frustrating. If your group is older—school age to teens—you might consider some of the more complicated construction sets that create a specific scene or building. Be sure you have all the proper materials and instructions before undertaking a family construction project.

Homemade Toys

These may seem very low tech for today's high-speed environment, but homemade toys are ideal for family play. They engage the family in a project, and the entire group can enjoy the fruits of the labor. Consider making your own homemade modeling dough, a scrapbook, or a bowling set from recyclable plastic soda bottles. Think through your project ahead of time so that you can collect any materials necessary. Also consider the age ranges in your group before picking a project. Be sure your choice will include all members of the family play group.

Family Toy Tips by Age and Stage

Perhaps the most critical ingredient to any family playtime is an understanding and appreciation of the ages involved. A toy choice that is made with all the ages and stages in mind—adults as well as children—has a much higher probability of success.

So if your family play group includes . . .

- *Babies:* choose toys that are safe for babies to handle—no small parts or loose strings that can cause injury. Understand that playtime may be short lived. Babies are not much for long attention spans. And plan family play around nap and feeding times. There's no point setting up a great family playtime session only to have baby burst into tears because he's hungry for dinner. Be mindful of baby's schedule.
- *Toddlers:* pick a familiar toy. Toddlers are creatures of habit. They are also very much into the "I do it myself!" phase, so a toy or game that they already know will head off having to deal with any frustrating learning curves. As with younger babies, be sure to plan family playtime carefully so as not to edge too close to meals or nap time. A toddler needs to be fed and well rested to enjoy any family activity, and play is no exception. Play that involves gross motor skills—as opposed to sitting quietly and taking turns—may appeal best to this group.
- *Preschoolers:* this age group is just about ready to participate in true family play—board games, puzzles,

construction projects, and the like—provided the toy is chosen properly. If you want a family board game, pick one that is highly visual and doesn't require reading skills so that the preschooler can play. A puzzle can be complicated, but set out a specific task, such as finding all the pieces that have blue on them, for your pre-school-age participants.

- **School-age kids:** often the best way to involve school-age children in family play is to pick a theme the children like. For example, a game or toy that revolves around a popular children's movie or show may be appealing. Also, at this age, children can be introduced to the notion of collecting, so family play that involves collectible dolls or trains or other items may be attractive. Consider the interests of your school-age child—is it sports or ballet or music?—and build family playtime around that theme to generate the most interest from young participants.

- **Teens:** it's tough to get teenagers to agree to family *anything;* this is the age when their friends seem so much cooler and more important. But you want to stay in their social hemisphere, so put some effort into picking family play items they will find tolerable. Technology may be a good choice here, appealing to the techno-savvy instincts of teens today. Also, many popular game and reality shows have developed related board games. That may help make a sale. If possible, look for a game that provides a bit of a challenge to your teen players; baby games will wear thin in a hurry. Be respectful when planning family playtime. Find time in the week when it will not keep your teen from something he or she finds far more appealing.

- ***Grandparents:*** we spend so much time and worry about how the children will cope that we often forget the older participants in family play. Grandparents will often be your most willing joiners. Many will very much want to engage in family playtime with children and grandchildren. But they also have needs. For example, toys and games that require knowledge of popular culture may be an area of difficulty. Not all grandparents are up on the latest tunes and teen idols. Also, games that require physical prowess or flexibility should also be carefully considered for age appropriateness. The goal is to have fun playing as a family. You'll want to pick a toy or game that everyone can enjoy without injury.

Timing Is Everything

When are you planning to schedule your family playtime? The choice of time and date does matter. The plan for a short nightly game is vastly different from the plan for a post-presents Christmas game date. The next sections look at the various times and their requirements.

Nightly

The key to a positive nightly experience is to choose a play element that doesn't take a lot of time. Look for an item that requires little or no setup and can be played with in a fun and satisfying manner in under twenty minutes. That's the best way to ensure that everyone—adults and children—will want to revisit the family playtime every night. If the playtime is too long or complicated, you'll all be tempted to let it slide.

TOY TIP

Story time is an excellent choice for nightly family playtime. With very young children, adults will need to read. As the kids grow, they can join in on the reading. To keep setup time to a minimum, create a basket of preselected books for nightly story time. That will speed the choice of material.

Weekly

Family playtime set for once a week calls for an activity that can easily fit into the life of a busy family yet at the same time stand apart from other play. Aim for a game or toy that will be slightly more complicated and longer in play. That will help distinguish this playtime from others during the week. Consider board games, puzzles, or construction sets.

Holiday Time

Holiday family playtime should be a special occasion. Break out the toys that might ordinarily sit untouched. A complicated construction project or puzzle may do well. A game that calls for team play may also be a good choice. This is also a time when collectibles may make a special appearance. Bringing out the family heirloom dolls, trains, or construction sets can enhance the enjoyment of special time with extended family.

TOY TIP

Don't feel as though you must schedule a weekly family playtime for the weekend. Although that's a time that often suits many families, others find weekends far too crowded with errands, sports, and other activities. What's more, weekends are prime social time for teens and even school-age children. They may find a weekend family playtime unwelcome on Saturday or Sunday. So be flexible. If Tuesday night is when everyone is free, that's fine. Or Friday before dinner. No day is better than another.

TOY TIP

If you're planning to try out some family playtime at your next gathering, don't keep it a secret. Let your relatives know what you have in mind. Consider sending out invitations (perhaps let the children make them) to clue everyone in on the planned activity. By getting everyone on board ahead of time, you reduce the play-delaying debate that may take place.

Vacation

Vacation time is memory-making time. To get the most out of your family playtime on vacation, look for activities or games that tie into your temporary surroundings. Are you in the country? Try a nature scavenger hunt. If you're by the water, incorporate water toys, games, and play into your family playtime. The games will be all the more memorable for their unique locations.

Snow Day

The words that children yearn for and parents dread: *snow day.* Your children may celebrate the day off from school or child care, but you must scramble to find something to occupy the troops for the day. Playing in the snow is obvious, but once that's over, what do you do with the children, who may range in age and are eager for organized fun? Snow days are great for homemade toys. The

 # TOY TIP

Everyone hopes the family vacation will be filled with sunshine, but every once in a while the weather just won't cooperate. So plan ahead for some rainy-day family playtime. Board games, card games, even a family video festival can help turn inclement weather into a family playtime opportunity.

TOY TIP

It's not easy to shop on a snow day, so try to have a secret stash of art and crafts supplies. Next time you're at the discount store, pick up some extra materials that you may need. Keep a box at home and toss in extra yarn, buttons, small boxes, and other items that you might one day press into craft-kit service. That way, when the snow is falling and the kids are whining, you can whip out the box stocked with supplies and be the snow day family hero.

activity can take up a good stretch of time because it incorporates first the making and then the playing. Consider homemade modeling dough, paper airplanes, collages, and other craft projects. Once the kids have completed the project, stage a presentation—an impromptu art gallery in the kitchen, a puppet show, or a dramatic scenario.

Conclusion

Family playtime is not the easiest to arrange, but it can be the most rewarding. For all the hours your child will spend with toys, the hours he or she can share toys with you will be the most memorable and the most valuable. Among the many things toys can teach is how to build and nurture a relationship. By sharing play with family, a child can learn to see toys as a way to connect with loved ones. That's a lesson that will last a lifetime.

WORKSHEET
Family Play Invites

The family that plays together stays together. But that playtime won't happen without some planning. To secure time in busy schedules, make and send family play invitations.

Come to Family Playtime!

Date:

Time:

What we'll play:

Who we'll play with:

RSVP and say you'll be there!

Tales from the Toy Tips Lab

When families engage in family playtime, they are doing more than playing. They are mastering and strengthening the ties that bind their particular clan. We've hosted many family game nights over the years to observe families in action. One night I remember well, we had one family that just would not leave. They kept playing and playing a board game. On closer observation I discovered why: Dad kept losing to his kids. And he really wanted to win, at least once. The children were happy to oblige, playing along until Dad won a round. Persistence, concentration, supporting your family member in pursuit of a goal—that's what that particular family displayed that night. The game was simply the pretext for the sharing of family values.

Chapter 11

Collectibles

Still fuming that Mom threw out your old base-ball card collection? Instead of dreaming about the millions that might have been, consider starting anew. Toy collections are increasingly popular—among children and adults. They can make great shared activities as both old and young delve into a particular toy specialty. Some people collect for fun, others for profit. It's a way to share a great toy experience with friends and family.

But toy collecting can also have a downside. Along with the popularity of the activity, ways to lose money on collecting are also on the rise. Many toy makers and sellers will promote their wares as surefire investments. Plenty of experts will claim to be accurate at spotting a future toy collectible treasure. There's a lot of opportunity for a toy collection habit to turn into a cash sink-hole. The keys to happy and successful toy collecting are smart, realistic planning and an ongoing quest for information and knowledge. They will help protect the young collector (and that collector's funds) from the hype machine.

The Basics of Collecting

Collecting can be confusing at first. Your best bet: tackle some of the commonly asked questions of collecting. Armed with the basics, you'll be on your way.

When Should You Introduce Collecting?

There's more than one school of thought on the best time to start a collection. Many parents with a passion for a particular item—perhaps trains or china dolls—will start a collection for a child. More than one infant has come into the world with a valuable toy collection well under way back in the nursery.

But if you take that route and begin any sort of collection when your child is a baby, be prepared to be the collection's caretaker for many years to come. School age is really the earliest a child can be counted on to maintain any sort of interest in collecting. Beware starting a collection around the interests of a toddler. They are fleeting. Toddlers and preschoolers can be passionate about trains one day, then bugs, then a cartoon character. It's the nature of this age to be curious about a range of things. So it's unwise to assume that even a strong interest on the part of a child under age five is the beginning of a lifelong love. It might be, but it also might be the flavor of the moment. If you invest in collections too early, you might be disappointed—and out a good deal of cash—when the child gets older and moves on to a new interest.

Once he or she gets to school age, a child is more mature and is better able to articulate true interests and passions, rather than just what is on his or her mind at the moment. At this stage, you can begin to introduce the idea of a collection. If you have collections of your own, you might consider showing them to your child, explaining how a collection may differ from the rest of the toys in the house. Children who develop an interest in collecting often do so because a parent or other adult in their lives shares the interest with them. So consider this part of a journey

TOY TIP

The collection may be the child's pride and joy, but it's still up to you to provide safe and appropriate play opportunities. Few children will be able to sit back and admire yet never touch a collection of toys. So make it possible for your child to play with his or her collectibles without junking the whole collection. For example, you may let the child have one or two items out at a time, or make a rule that playtime with the collection must take place with an adult present.

your child may take with you or a grandparent or other relative. Collecting is an activity best shared.

Whose Collection Is It?

There is an important point for you, the adult, to ponder. Whose collection is it, anyway? You'll want to think this through and set the appropriate ground rules for your child.

Is It Primarily the Child's Collection?   In this case, you'll want to be available to provide guidance and support, but ultimately this is an effort driven by your child's interests and commitment. Avoid becoming overly involved in the decisions surrounding the collection. This is a project for which your child may develop a sense of ownership and pride.

Is It a Shared Collection?   These are often very rewarding collections—projects maintained in equal parts by a child and a parent or other treasured adult. The most important elements to success in this kind of collection are shared interests and tasks. At first, the tasks may separate out based on age appropriateness. After all, a grade-schooler can't be expected to contribute half the money necessary to maintain the collection. But a portion of the funds can come from the child if you are indeed setting up the collection as a partnership. Share decision making about display, acquisition, and research. Build in your child a sense that the two of you are a team on a shared mission.

Is It Really Your Collection?   Be honest, especially those of you who started the child's collection when he or she was still in utero: Is the toy collection really *your* pas-

 TOY TIP

Set aside special times to manage and enjoy a shared collection. This is more than just a toy collection. It's a connection point between adult and child. If you set aside a particular time to spend with the child on the collection, that special significance will be hammered home. It need not be every day or every week. The time spent on the collection can revolve around family holidays, school vacations, and other more irregularly occurring moments. By carving out time, you send the message that the collection—and the collector—are special.

TOY TIP

Store your collection someplace where it will not be a temptation to tiny hands. It's difficult for a child—especially one younger than five—to appreciate that there are toys in the world not meant to be played with. If you intend to keep your collection pristine, take appropriate storage measures. If your child shows an interest, you may begin to teach the skills of the careful collector around school age. But continue to treat your collection as a hands-off valuable until you are certain your child can appreciate the difference between toys and collectibles.

sion? That's not uncommon. Many adults maintain a significant and extensive toy collection, and that's a great hobby. But if it would break your heart if your child damaged an item in your collection, be wise and don't share the collection until your child is old enough and careful enough to respect your treasured property. No child wants to be the one who busted Dad's favorite collectible.

What's It All About?

All great collections have a theme. Not just a theme that defines the content of the collections—such as die-cast cars or painted soldiers—but a theme that explains what the purpose of the collection really is in the life of its owner. Different collections have different missions. Understanding the reason your child has a collection can help you guide your young collector to a successful and fulfilling experience.

What's It For?

By understanding the goal of the collection, you'll be better able to help your child enjoy it.

Acquisition   For this collector, the thrill is in the hunt. The child may love perusing stores, yard sales, websites, and classifieds searching for the perfect addition to a burgeoning collection. The entertainment factor is not so much in the having as in the seeking. You can help this acquisition-minded collector by arranging appropriate shopping trips, showing the child the many news and research resources available to collectors, even by subscribing to catalogues and other sources of information and photographs. Keep close tabs on the amount you are willing to spend—or willing to let your child spend as he or she grows up and has more access to personal funds. Consider setting specific limits.

Parental role: your key contribution to this kind of collection will be knowledge of retail. A child won't understand the ins and outs of merchant mania, so you'll have to be the one who can make the decisions on when, where, and how to shop for collectible items. This may require some learning on your part. Traditional retail stores may offer what your child wants and needs, or you may find yourself looking into fairs, trade shows, and other more specific outlets. Also, you'll want to educate yourself on the issues of pricing. Again, a child may not understand when he or she is being ripped off; being a watchdog will be your role. Consider investing in an up-to-date price guide and carrying it with you when you and your child hit the stores or other shopping venues.

Investing (Long Term)   Many collectors—even young ones—dream that one day their treasure will be worth a lot of money. Baseball cards, stamp collections, dolls based on movie stars, TV show lunch boxes—all have seen glory days in which the item, once viewed as an inexpensive child's plaything, gains value over the years to be a true moneymaker. Education and realistic expectations are the keys to happiness as a long-term investment collector. Teach your child about the true economics of toy collecting. Get information from auctions, online trading sites, and printed materials that can give an accurate picture of how much a toy can be worth   and how long it takes to achieve that value.

Parental role: you may think your role in the building of this kind of collection is to understand the financial possibilities of collectibles, but in fact, that type of knowledge is decidedly secondary. More important, you'll need to ramp up your expertise in the subject of storage. Proper storage is often what makes the difference between a truly valuable collection and a damaged box of old toys. If you are really thinking of this collection as a long-term investment, understand the special storage considerations of the collectibles your child has chosen. Dolls, for example, should not be stored in vinyl cases without other protection, such as acid-free paper or even old cloth diapers. Items that come in particular packaging, such as action figures in plastic bubble cards, must be stored so that the plastic material doesn't bend or crack.

Display   Many toy collections are serious works of art. A burgeoning collection can make for wonderful decoration. If your child finds the visual aspects of the collection most appealing, you can help by providing appropriate places for display and storage. These may be in the child's room on special shelving or wall space or in a more public area of the family home, depending on the nature of the collection. After all, a lovely doll collection may look great in the family room, but you might not be as enamored with the latest in science fiction trading cards. Use your judgment and discuss it with your child. Any display case must be safe for children. Your child may try to access it when you are not in the room. Cases with glass doors or other potential hazards must be carefully inspected and fitted for safety.

Parental role: your primary task is that of furniture coordinator. If your child wants to display his or her collectibles, it will be up to you to purchase and arrange the appropriate container. That may be something as easy as a low-rise bookshelf or as complex as a storage cabinet with florescent lighting. To make that call you'll need to consider your child's interest and the nature of the collection.

Trading and Selling (Short Term)   Although some children may be willing to hold on to a collection for years and years, others may be eager to jump into the fray of trading and selling right away. For these children, a quick course in business practices is in order. A child that will be trading with other children needs to understand the rules of fair trading. What constitutes cheating? What is a "good" trade versus a "bad" trade? How should you conduct yourself when trading with your peers, and when do you need to tap a grown-up to intervene? As the parent, you must talk about these questions with your young collector. Learning to trade in a fair manner is an important aspect of character development, and collecting is a great opportunity to broach this subject.

Parental role: this is your child's entry into the word of commerce, and your job is to prepare him or her to behave appropriately. Often trades and other deals go down without an adult present. Because you won't be on site to supervise your child's actual transactions, it's important to specifically discuss ground rules with him or her. Talk about fair trades and the importance of honest behavior and good business practices. This may seem like dry material for a child, but it is the bedrock of this aspect of character education. Also help your child learn to recognize a bad deal or a poor trade and what to do or say to avoid that type of situation.

Playing   Many children may want to collect a particular item for the sole purpose of playing with it—right now. They collect a type of toy not to place it on a shelf, trade it for profit, or save it as an investment but to get down on the floor and enjoy it in the here and now. As the older and wiser participant, you may see this as short-term thinking. But if this is your child's goal as a collector, it's wise to support it rather than fight it. If you encourage your child to collect but then refuse to let him or her open the packaging or play with the toys, that child may simply lose interest in the whole thing. So if your child wants to play with his or her collectibles, you can explain the ramifications, but allow some actual playtime.

Parental role: although you don't want to sack all the fun by locking up the collection in a vault, it's your job to educate your child as to the relative pros and cons of treating a collectible the way one might treat any other toy. Even after you have done so, your child may opt to bring the toy out for playtime anyway. But as children get older, they often begin to recognize the big picture. Establish yourself as a source of information that your child can turn to when it comes to collectibles. Furnish your child with age-appropriate reference materials, for example, to help teach the value of collectibles.

What Makes a Great Collection?

There are no hard-and-fast rules about what kinds of toys make the best collectibles. It depends greatly on the interest of the child and the availability of collectible product. Toys with classic appeal often make great collectibles. These are toys that have some history behind them but are not so old-fashioned as to be dull. Dolls, trains, cars, and other familiar toys all fall into this category. These offer good collectible fun because they have long and storied histories. At the same time, they are in current production, so there is always something new and interesting coming onto the scene.

What Makes a Disappointing Collection?

The black hole of the collectible business can be summed up in one word: *fads.* The hot toy, the must-have category, the thing all the kids are talking about this week. Whatever it is, it may seem like a natural collectible, but in many cases it's a fad and will be over and done with in six months. That's not always the case. Certainly there are great collectibles that started out as fads. But most fad items come and go, and keeping and saving a big old box

of them is a waste of money and space. How can you spot
a fad? Ask yourself these questions:

- *Is it inexpensive and mass produced?* Very few
  great collectibles come via the fast-food industry or
  other quick-stop distribution method.
- *Is it connected to a television show or movie?*
  These passions are often short lived. Kids will move on
  to the next entertainment theme as soon as Hollywood
  churns it out. So collecting cards or merchandise related to an entertainment product should be considered
  a short-term, play-now program rather than an investment in a true collection.
- *Does it lack intergenerational appeal?* Sure, there's
  a first time for everything, and it's possible that the new
  item your child loves is the start of a huge collectible
  trend. But most great collections have some element
  that appeals to a variety of generations. That's often
  why classic toys trump newcomers in the collectibles
  business.

The Hidden Benefits of Toy Collecting

There are many educational and social benefits to maintaining a specialized toy collection. You might not care to
overemphasize these benefits with your child—he or she
might see collecting as too much like a school assignment
in disguise. But you can be aware of them yourself and
help support the learning as well as the collecting.

- *Collecting teaches long-term thinking.* Many toys
  are based firmly in the here and now of a child's life. A
  collection encourages a child to think long term.

- *Collecting promotes family connections.* Whether you start a collection with your child or a child receives a collection handed down from a parent or grandparent, collectibles forge a link between generations. Often a child will learn more about what life was like long ago from the collectibles than from any book.

- *Collectibles teach character.* Collectibles are often sold on the gray markets: auction sites, yard sales, and school yards. These are places where official rules are often ignored and deals are struck among interested parties. Your child will encounter challenges to his or her honesty and integrity. Honesty is an important character issue, and collectibles provide a good platform to discuss it with your child.

- *Collectibles support many academic subjects.* The various activities involved in collecting can teach social history, math skills, and organizational and research skills. These all have very real and practical applications in the classroom.

Conclusion

Collectibles offer children a preview of adult life. They teach business skills and show the value of patience, persistence, hard work, and research. They underscore the notion that some wonderful things in life take many, many years to evolve before the final payoff. Although they are a high-maintenance category of toys, collectibles also bring joys and educational elements few other playthings can match.

WORKSHEET

What's Your Collectibles Quotient?

Take this quick true-or-false quiz.

1. Toys gain value only if kept in their original packaging.
2. Collectibles with misprints, packaging errors, and other manufacturing mistakes are very valuable.
3. Collectibles should be stored in natural light.
4. A child can play with his or her collectibles.
5. You should collect in a "niche."
6. Reputable collectibles dealers have return policies.
7. Financial gain, not personal preference, should drive collections.
8. Old cloth diapers are good for storing collectible dolls.
9. Hot movies often generate valuable collectibles.
10. If a potential collectible breaks, it's worthless.

Answers:

1F   2F   3F   4T   5T   6T   7F   8T   9F   10F

Tales from the Toy Tips Lab

As a toy professional, I am often approached by friends, family, and colleagues with eager questions about the value of their treasured toys from childhood. So many people come up and ask me, "I still have my favorite [doll, action figure, baseball card, race car—you name it] from childhood. What's it worth?" And I always respond, "It's worth the joyful memories you have of playing with the toy. Nothing you can get in cash could equal that."

Chapter 12

Classic Toys

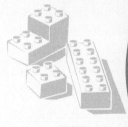

Toyland is an industry in constant flux. Often what is wildly hot one year will disappear from view the next. It's not the sort of industry you get into if your goal is slow growth and longevity. But for every rule, there are exceptions, and in the toy industry, those who buck the traditional system enter a small but high-profile category: the classics.

What is a true classic toy? Marketers like to throw the term *classic* around quite a bit, but the basic definition of a classic toy is that it has survived on toy shelves continuously for more than one generation. So if you played with it and it's still around when you go out shopping for your kids, you have yourself a classic. Some super-classics stretch back more than one generation to the earliest incarnations of mass production and distribution of playthings. They are truly rare. Most classics are two-generation wonders. And even lasting two generations is a major achievement, especially when you consider the fleeting attention span of the average child.

Fortunately, classic toys often get some help from the economic cycle. When times are flush, new gadgets and creations get all the attention. But when recession looms and consumers look to get the most value for their toy dollars, classic toys often make a comeback. That's when shoppers are less willing to risk an unknown and fall back on the toys with track records. Classics endure for many reasons, and economic hard times are one of them. When you're pinching pennies, you don't want to make a mistake, and two generations of longevity don't lie.

Key Classic Categories

Where can you find the classics? Many of the leading classic toys come from just a handful of key toy categories.

Board Games

By far the largest selection of classics can be found in this aisle. From Parcheesi to Sorry! to Monopoly, board games have been some of the most enduring playthings in the modern history of toys. Today, thanks to consolidation in the toy industry, many of these classic board games are housed under the same corporate umbrella—Hasbro. But at the time of their invention—as far back as 1867 for Parcheesi—they were created and launched by fierce game-making rivals. The simplicity of the rules and the appeal to a range of ages has helped make board games popular through history. Although marketers may try to jump-start sales by introducing new, improved, or anniversary editions of these classics, the originals remain popular.

Construction Sets

Whether made of traditional wood or modern plastics, building and construction toys have produced a large selection of classic toys. Some are items with broad appeal, such as Lincoln Logs and Tinker Toys. Others are meant for older kids or even playful adults, such as the famous Erector Set. And then there are construction toys that revamped their industry, such as LEGO. More than a construction toy, LEGO revolutionized construction toys with its look, materials, and ability to inspire generations of builders.

Vehicles

Planes, trains, and automobiles have inspired more than their fair share of classic toys. Some, like Lionel trains, are true collectibles. Others, like Matchbox and Hot Wheels, are meant for full-time play in the here and now. Generations of children have pushed vehicles across the kitchen floor and dreamed of speeding down the highway in a race car or soaring in the wild blue yonder in a two-engine prop. Although this category has been infused with technology, leading to the creation of many newcomers, the classics endure because they fuel the imagination of the child traveler.

Dolls

Dolls are relative youngsters to the world of classic toys. Certainly there have been dolls for generations, and many different brands among collectibles, but when it comes to everyday dolls meant to be played with and enjoyed rather than displayed, they have not traditionally inspired a wide selection of classics. In recent generations, that has changed as toy makers have come up with true personalities and back stories for their doll offerings. This has led to the rise of such classics as Barbie, the Cabbage Patch Kids, and even G.I. Joe. These dolls made the generational leap not just because they're fun but because they came complete with personality.

Technology Toys

There are genuine classics in the category of technology toys. Surprised? Don't be. The key is to remember the year in which they debuted. View-Master was a marvel of 3-D fun in 1938, its launch year. Etch-a-Sketch broke new technological ground in 1960. The Easy-Bake Oven was cutting-edge in 1963. Although their technologies may seem tame by today's virtual-reality standards, in their day they were techno-wonders.

Why Classic Toys?

With so many new toys on the market each year, why bother with the old-timers? After all, these classics are probably not the items kids are clamoring for. They're more apt to be asking for what they've seen on TV. But that doesn't mean you should overlook classic toys. In fact, there are several situations in which classic toys trump their new competition as better picks. Consider the following scenarios.

Family Playtime

Classic toys are clear winners in the family playtime category. Why? Because everyone will know how to play. When you bring out a classic board game or construction toy,

 TOY TIP

Ask the older members of your family to suggest classic toys or games for family play. There are some great classic toys that you may inadvertently overlook. So poll the senior members of your family play group and see what they recall as their best and most fun playthings. You may find you already have them in the toy box, just waiting for the opportunity to come out and play.

multiple generations will recognize and have experience with that very toy. That means no downtime while one family member tries to learn the rules of an unfamiliar game. When you're planning family play, be sure to consider classic toys. They help get the fun started quickly and are an excellent way for older generations to share memories with the younger set.

Gift-Buying Time

You may find yourself in the toy aisles in need of a gift for a child you don't know well or for a friend of your own child. You may not know the child's family all that well either. In these situations, the difficulty of choosing is compounded. Classic toys are a safe haven in these cases, or when you're buying for a child with strict family rules surrounding toy choices.

 TOY TIP

To bridge the gap between parents who may appreciate a classic toy and kids who want something more modern, try some themed versions of classic toys. Many classic games and dolls are now available in licensed versions—they may incorporate the characters or colors of a popular TV show or movie. The familiar theme helps connect the child to the classic game.

Teaching Time

There may be periods in your life as a parent when you'll want to teach your child any number of life lessons: how to win and lose graciously, how to take turns, and how to work together in a team, among others. A classic toy often serves as a good venue for these discussions. Your familiarity with the toy will help you guide the play toward the discussion you'd like to have with your child. A toy you know less well may require more of your concentration and leave you less focused on the educational lesson you're hoping to impart.

Classics Through the Ages

When should you introduce classic toys? That depends on the toy and the age of the child. Some classics are appropriate early on; others require an older child's skill. But there are classic opportunities for every age group.

 # TOY TIP

Try to be a bit subtle in your teaching efforts. Although you may want to get your message across as quickly as possible, if the child senses that this is really lecture time, not playtime, the jig is up. So look for ways to make your teaching point without bulldozing over the fun of playing together with your child.

Babies

Teddy bears are a good choice for tiny ones; just be sure the teddy you choose is safe for an infant. That means no small parts or detachable items. Ideally, features should be sewn on rather than glued, and the teddy should be small enough so as not to present a suffocation hazard. Cute as a teddy bear may seem, don't place it in a crib with an infant under six months of age. Babies that young should not be left unsupervised with any toy, even a teddy bear.

Toddlers

Break out the perennial toddler favorite—Mr. Potato Head. Since his debut in 1952 he's been entertaining little ones as they marvel at the mystery of the ever-changing face. Vehicles also make excellent classic choices for this age group. Toddlers are just learning the concept of cause and effect, and nothing drives that home quite like a toy car. For toddler-parent playtime, you might also consider such classics as the Radio Flyer wagon.

Preschool

At this age, children are ready for the biggest category of classic toys: the board game. You may want to start out with Candyland, which requires no reading skills; its basic color-coded rules are still popular with each new crop of three-year-olds to come along. Also great for preschoolers are art toys, such as Play-Doh, and construction toys, such as LEGO.

School Age

At this age, children are able to try some of the more complicated classics. For the methodical builder, try a first Erector Set. The yo-yo, first introduced by Duncan in 1929, is also a good pick. Such strategy classics as Clue, Stratego, and Battleship can join the mix. And if your household can't handle a puppy, consider the Original Ant Farm—placating pet demands since 1956.

Preteens

Classics offer some appealing items even to this finicky, eye-rolling, "That is *so boring*" age group. Scrabble, Sorry!, Beat the Clock, and Concentration may all be challenging enough to keep the interest of an older child. And if you really want to leverage a classic toy for educational purposes, there's always the Game of Life.

Where to Shop

Classic toys make their home at a number of different retailers.

- *Discount stores.* Although a discount chain may not carry every toy, it is likely to carry the classics because they have broad appeal and can be counted on to sell reasonably well.
- *Toy chains.* Toy superstores may promote the newest items, but they're still stocking the classic toys. Ask if you don't see them.

- **Bookstores.** As booksellers seek to expand their customer base, many are now offering toys in their children's sections. Classics are often popular with this retail segment. That's especially true if the classic toy has any literary presence—for example, a series or picture book based on the characters.
- **Specialty stores.** Although this is not the only place to locate classic toys, it is often the best place if you're on the hunt for a hard-to-find classic, such as the anniversary edition of a particular toy or game, or a high-end deluxe edition of the toy.
- **Online.** Like discount stores, Internet merchants are going to stock what's selling. Classic toys may not appear on the first page of a Web-based store, but fire up the search engine and look.
- **Department stores.** Department stores used to have regular toy departments as part of their merchandise mix. Today, many have given up on selling toys so as to free the space for more profitable items. But come the holiday season, many department stores set up temporary Christmas sections. They often feature classic toys, especially dolls and vehicles.

Myths About Classic Toys

- **They're better than the newcomers.** No, not better. Just different. They may be less complex or more enduring in their fun quotient. But there are many excellent new toys on the market, some of them destined to be classics themselves. The designation of *classic* just means the toy has stood the test of time.
- **They're more educational than newer toys.** Not so. In fact, many newer toys can be better suited to

today's educational challenges. Toys developed in an earlier generation may not meet the academic standards of today's classroom.

- *They're less commercial.* Wow, that's a miss. These toys of yesteryear get just as much promotion as their newer cousins—maybe more. Maybe you won't see them paired with your child's fast-food meal, but they are definitely part of the media mix. Updated television commercials pitch many of these classic games on children's television shows. And marketers are quick to leverage a toy's "classic" status in advertising.

- *They're better made and of better quality.* Sometimes yes, sometimes no. Many classic toys are now owned by toy manufacturing conglomerates, so their quality will be similar to other wares of that larger firm. Many of the classics were originally the creations of independent toy makers, but today, most classic toys are part of a large stable. Quality will be reflected companywide, not in the classic toy alone.

How Can Classics Compete?

With all the products out there today that can grip a child's imagination and attention, how can you ever hope to engage your little one in play with a classic? Follow these tips:

- *Play together.* Don't just hand your child a classic toy and hope for the best. Make sure you play with it together. Your involvement will enhance the stature of the toy in your child's eyes.

- *Share your memories.* If this is a toy you loved as a child, tell your child about your experience. A classic toy can provide a great moment of connection between generations.

- ***Be prepared to answer the "old toys are boring!" complaint.*** Ask your child to try it with you, or explain your reasons for wanting to play with this particular toy. If your child is in a challenging stage, be ready with your answer.

Conclusion

Classic toys are a true gift to the weary parent. They are like old friends when we are overwhelmed by the multitude of toy choices, and they continue to entertain us year after year. In a world that seems to move and change so quickly and constantly, classic toys remind us that good ideas have staying power and that great toys are still with us.

Top-Rated Classics, by Age and Stage

Over the years, Toy Tips has tested many thousands of toys. What follows are the classic toys that have shown the best results.

- *Infants*
  Chatter Phone (Fisher-Price)
  Little People Animal Sounds Farm (Fisher-Price)

- *Toddlers*
  Corn Popper (Fisher-Price)
  Little People Fun Sounds Garage (Fisher-Price)
  Sit 'n Spin (Hasbro)
  Dressy Bessy (Hasbro)
  Dapper Dan (Hasbro)

- ***Preschool***
  Ants in the Pants (Hasbro)
  Candyland (Hasbro)
  Guess Who? (Hasbro)
  Lite-Brite (Hasbro)
  Mousetrap (Hasbro)
  The Original Husker Du (Pressman Toy Corp.)
  Silly Putty (Binney & Smith Inc.)

- ***School Age***
  Battleship (Hasbro)
  Boggle (Hasbro)
  Clue (Hasbro)
  Colorforms (University Games)
  Connect Four (Hasbro)
  Ker Plunk (Mattel)
  Trouble (Hasbro)
  Sorry! (Hasbro)
  The Game of Life (Hasbro)
  Uno (Mattel)
  Yahtzee (Hasbro)
  Concentration (Endless Games)

WORSHEET

The Toy Tips Challenge

How much do you know about classic toys? Test your savvy.

1. *Jenga* is a Swahili word meaning
   a. to build
   b. to concentrate
   c. to play together
   d. to dance
2. Yahtzee was originally called
   a. Chutes and Ladders
   b. Risk
   c. Trouble
   d. Yacht Game
3. Which toy was a popular fad with children and adults during the 1980s?
   a. Jack in the box
   b. Sit 'n Spin
   c. Rubik's Cube
   d. The Green Machine
4. Which construction toy can be connected 1,060 different ways with only three pieces?
   a. Erector Set
   b. LEGO
   c. Lincoln Logs
   d. K'nex
5. What product has already celebrated its fiftieth anniversary?
   a. Barbie
   b. Cootie
   c. Little People
   d. Lincoln Logs

6. Whose son designed and developed Lincoln Logs?
   a. Paul Klee
   b. John F. Kennedy
   c. Frank Lloyd Wright
   d. Pablo Picasso
7. What was the first product ever advertised on television?
   a. Slinky
   b. Mr. Potato Head
   c. Chatty Cathy
   d. Play-Doh
8. How many pounds of yellow paint does it take to make Tonka trucks each year?
   a. 2,330
   b. 14,144
   c. 52,400
   d. 83,045
9. In one year, Lionel made nearly one million engines, cabooses, and other rolling stock. That would make a toy train nearly 180 miles long. If it were a real train, how long would it be?
   a. 2,000 miles
   b. 5,500 miles
   c. 7,000 miles
   d. 28,000 miles
10. Matchbox toy cars have over one hundred vehicles in the line and are still priced around $1.00. In what year were they first developed?
   a. 1905
   b. 1942
   c. 1952
   d. 1977

Answers:

1. A. As a child, the creator of Jenga lived in Africa, where she spoke Swahili. In Swahili, *jenga* means "to build." Jenga—Parker Brothers.

2. D. Yahtzee was invented in 1956 by a Canadian couple aboard their yacht. It was dubbed their "Yacht game." They approached a Bingo manufacturer about printing copies of the game as gifts, and Yahtzee was born. Yahtzee—Parker Brothers.

3. C. In 1982, one of every three American homes had at least one, causing the term *Rubik's Cube* to become an entry in the *Oxford English Dictionary.* Rubik's Cube—Milton Bradley.

4. B. Three eight-stud LEGO bricks can be combined in 1,060 different ways. Six eight-stud LEGO bricks can be combined in 102,987,500 different ways. LEGO—LEGO Systems.

5. C. Little People were once stationary figures on the Looky Fire Truck; it took nine years for them to gain their independence. Little People—Fisher-Price.

6. C. John Lloyd Wright, son of Frank Lloyd Wright, created Lincoln Logs after seeing construction techniques used by his dad for an earthquake-proof hotel in Tokyo. Lincoln Logs—K'nex.

7. B. Introduced in 1952, Mr. Potato Head profited from a new sales tool—television commercials. This toy grossed $4 million in its very first year. Mr. Potato Head—Hasbro.

8. B. More than 240 million trucks have been manufactured since 1947. It takes 14,144 pounds of yellow paint and 5.5 million pounds (2,478 tons) of sheet metal a year to make Tonka trucks and other Tonka vehicles. Tonka—Hasbro.

9. C. The first electrical Lionel train was designed for a window display in New York. If the engines and cars were real, they would make a train over 7,000 miles long. Lionel trains—Lionel LLC.

10. C. The Matchbox was born in 1952, when John Odell created a brass prototype of a Road Roller and put it in a small box for his daughter. Matchbox—Mattel.

 ## Tales from the Toy Tips Lab

One of the best guides to great toys and satisfying play is the parents' own memories of childhood. As I was growing up, I often read books and shared my own stories with my parents. Today, I share that same experience with my son. My time with him is enhanced by the fact that I have my own fond memories of this very type of play. There are wonderful new playthings on the market today. But parents should combine these new items with their own favorites from childhood.

About the Authors

*M*arianne M. Szymanski is founder and president of Toy Tips, Inc., a child development research group that conducts independent ongoing academic research on products from the toy and juvenile product industries. A national author, entrepreneur, speaker, lecturer, and media personality, Marianne has led her organization's unbiased tests of over thirty-four thousand products from more than nine hundred manufacturers.

Marianne created the Toy Research Institute and leads the industry with her independent and unbiased review process. A former retail sales representative for an international toy manufacturer, Marianne saw the opportunity to provide parents with unbiased information they can trust on how to select products that enhance a child's development. This inspired the formation in 1991 of The Toy Research Institute, a year-round evaluation program that does not accept revenue from manufacturers for the review process.

Marianne holds a dual degree in psychology and marketing from Marquette University. She is married to Garo Hartounian. They live in Milwaukee, Wisconsin, with their son, Maximillian. More information is available at www.toytips.com.

Ellen Neuborne is a veteran business journalist with more than a dozen years on the retail and marketing beat. She has covered seven Toy Fairs, fourteen Christmas shopping seasons, and countless consumer fads from Ninja Turtles to Razor Scooters. She's covered the toy industry for *USA Today, BusinessWeek,* and Americanbaby.com. Her work has also appeared in *Working Mother, Inc.,* and *Ms.* She holds a B.A. in classics from Brown University. She's married to fellow journalist David Landis. They live in New York City with their two children, Henry and Leslie.